GUNBOAT DIPLOMACY
1895–1905

Great Power Pressure in Venezuela

MIRIAM HOOD, M.A., Ph.D.

London
GEORGE ALLEN & UNWIN
Boston   Sydney

George Allen & Unwin (Publishers) Ltd,
40 Museum Street, London WC1A 1LU, UK

George Allen & Unwin (Publishers) Ltd,
Park Lane, Hemel Hempstead, Herts HP2 4TE, UK

Allen & Unwin, Inc.,
9 Winchester Terrace, Winchester, Mass. 01890, USA

George Allen & Unwin Australia Pty Ltd,
8 Napier Street, North Sydney, NSW 2060, Australia

First published in 1975
Second edition 1983

Transcripts of Crown Copyright Records in the Public Record
Office appear by permission of the Controller of Her Majesty's
Stationery Office.

British Library Cataloguing in Publication Data

Hood, Miriam.
  Gunboat diplomacy.
  1. Venezuela – Foreign relations   2. Venezuela – History –
Anglo-German Blockade, 1902
I. Title
327.87   F2325
ISBN 0-04-987002-5

Library of Congress Cataloging in Publication Data

Hood, Miriam
  Gunboat diplomacy, 1895–1905
Bibliography: p.
Includes index.
1. Venezuela – History – Anglo-German Blockade, 1902.
2. Venezuela – Foreign relations.   3. Venezuela – Politics and government
– 1830–1935.   I. Title.
F2325.H66 1983   987'.062   83–2744
ISBN 0-04-987002-5

Printed in Great Britain by Biddles Ltd, Guildford, Surrey

Preface

Imperial Great Britain was less active in Latin America than in any other part of the world. Only three spots of red showed on the map to the south and west of the Caribbean: British Honduras, British Guiana and the Falkland Islands. These were not ruled by viceroys, nor did they offer brilliant prospects to civil servants, or great fortunes to merchants. We had a substantial trade with Latin America, and were the leading foreign investors in most parts up until the First World War, but business was carried on by only a small number of resident British. We had, on the whole, a peaceful time too. We invaded the River Plate in 1806 and 1807, but did not repeat the aberration after an ignominious defeat. We blockaded the same river ineffectually in 1845–6. We joined the French in threatening Mexico in 1861–2, but quickly abandoned them when their adventure went further. Ships from the Royal Navy provided at other times and places a hint about this or that incident, or a hint that no incident should occur.

From the imperial centre, none of this fired the British imagination at the time, or remained in the memory later. Yet it is no coincidence that our direct presence left three diplomatic problems that are not yet solved. British Honduras has become Belize, and has differences with Guatemala. British Guiana has now full independence as Guayana, but Venezuela has claims on the Essequibo region. According to the 1966 Geneva Agreement, to which Great Britain is a signatory, these claims are to be settled by a negotiation that is yet to take place. We were reminded of the Falkland Islands in 1982.

The timely reappearance of Miriam Hood's *Gunboat Diplomacy 1895–1905* recalls another event that is here largely forgotten, the Anglo-German blockade of Venezuela in 1902–3. Sra. Blanco Fombona de Hood is the bearer of a great Venezuelan name, and for many years she has been Cultural Counsellor at the Venezuelan Embassy in London, a post she has filled with a passion for getting Venezuela known and a tenacity in getting the British to pay attention that shows no signs of diminishing. She therefore writes in a spirit rather different from that which would come easiest to a British historian, who might see the blockade as a marginal, atypical occurrence, interesting perhaps as a sort of marker in Anglo-US relations, perhaps as a 'case-history' (condescending phrase), but not something to be remembered as Venezuelans remember it. The British historian of Empire could be right in his way, but his version would not be complete, and he would fail to convey much of what *Gunboat Diplomacy 1895–1905* says and implies.

Events we have forgotten are not necessarily all-forgotten elsewhere. In the South Atlantic conflict, Venezuela was Argentina's most decided supporter among all Latin American nations. The two countries had different systems of government. They had in common territorial disputes that derived from nineteenth-century British activity. They also, as Miriam Hood shows, shared memories of that bizarre blockade of eighty years ago. In 1902 Luis Maria Drago, the Argentine Foreign Minister, in communications to the US Secretary of State, condemned this type of pressure, and his condemnation forms the basis of the 'Drago Doctrine' on such intervention, a significant Latin American contribution to international law. This was a gesture of solidarity that Venezuela repaid in 1982.

There are other things to learn from these pages – something of Guzmán Blanco, something of our successive Ministers in Caracas, of the interactions of bond-holders and governments, of Anglo-American differences on the Guiana boundary question, of Grover Cleveland's and Theodore Roosevelt's elaboration on the Monroe Doctrine. Miriam Hood may not have said the last word on any of these, but she awakens our all-too-dormant interest. More importantly, the reader of this short work will see that there is a Latin-American way of looking at not-so-distant history, that does not come naturally to us, but that it is neither polite nor wise to ignore.

Malcolm Deas
St Antony's College, Oxford

Foreword

❧

It could well puzzle the reader that the subject of Gunboat Diplomacy, events which took place at the beginning of the twentieth century, should in any way be linked to the present border dispute between Venezuela and Guiana. The events in the South Atlantic during 1982 make it particularly relevant since that tragic war was the result of prolonged misunderstanding and the protagonists not knowing or appreciating each other's point of view.

The Anglo-German Blockade, which is the subject of this book, was likewise the outcome of misunderstanding between two peoples. This must not happen again. That is why I have included a summary of a speech by Venezuela's Foreign Secretary, Dr Zambrano, regarding Venezuela's position over her Essequibo claim.

'There is a wind of change' in the words of a former British Prime Minister. Indeed since the beginning of the century Great Britain has been the chief protagonist making this possible. Her record in giving her former colonies independence is unequalled and her insistence in proclaiming peace and justice constant. That is why I believe that justice must in the end prevail regarding Venezuela's claim to the Essequibo and the more people are aware of it, the better chance we have that a peaceful solution will be found.

Venezuela's claim to the Essequibo is not a recent one as many imply. In the words of Dr Zambrano: 'This situation was accepted by England, when in 1824, upon recognising the independence of Great Colombia, it identified the new state with the following expression – this beautiful and rich country which extends through the northern sea from the Essequibo river to the province of Guiana.'

The wind of change which has so successfully blown away the old colonialism is a mark of the last decades of the twentieth century. Rarely in world history has there been such international pre-occupation with human rights and the ideals of justice and peace as there is now. We believe the 21st century will find the continent of Latin America playing a vital role in world affairs.

Gunboat Diplomacy

The border dispute between two sister nations such as Venezuela and Guiana must influence the course of history and its importance is, I am afraid, not sufficiently appreciated. The gunboat diplomacy which took place at the beginning of this century is more than outmoded, as will be seen from the following chapters. That is why, since to know is to understand, I have no hesitation in repeating Dr Zambrano's statement regarding Venezuela's position over the border dispute. Again I quote: 'we are a country which has earned the respect of the international community through our inevitable attachment to the cause of justice and right as the axis for international relations . . .'. Because of Latin America's ever growing importance it is necessary for a student of these events to take stock of our failures in the past and to hope that by a better understanding of our history we will reach a peaceful and just solution to differences between countries and the unity of Latin America.

Contents

vii

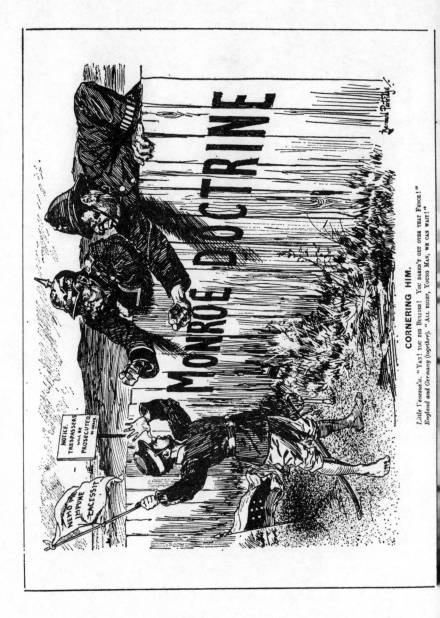

CORNERING HIM.

Little Venezuela. "Yah! you big Bullies! You darsn't get over that Fence!"
England and Germany (together). "All right, Young Man, we can wait!"

Chapter 1

❧❧

Introduction

'I blush to say it,' wrote Bolivar, 'but independence is the only benefit we have gained at the cost of everything else.' Mensaje al Congreso Constituyente de la Republica de Colombia, 20 January 1830, *Obras Completas*, **ii**, 1275.

The Spanish spirit has two faces, like Janus in Roman mythology. One aspect is that of fortitude: it is stoical and fatalistic—the other despises everything: this is the Spaniard's mystical side.[1] The Venezuelan of the nineteenth century had much in common with his Spanish forebears. He had his fortitude and his stoicism. He despised all. But here the similarities end. The Spaniard, when he despised material goods, did so because he was a mystic. The Venezuelan condemned them because he believed passionately in equality. The key to Venezuela's history may be found in this passion for equality. Nothing has ever moved the Venezuelan people as much, and their turbulent history reflects this. It is this idea of equality which made possible the barbarous wars, and the rise and fall of the Venezuelan caudillo. During the second part of the nineteenth century, sociological and political reasons motivated this feverish quest, the *leit-motiv* of the period.

During the second half of the nineteenth century, the great international events made little internal impact on Venezuela. She was still an isolated country, insignificant in the universal economy. She lived a life apart from the living where criollan and traditional institutes were more powerful than foreign

---

[1] Rufino Blanco-Fombona, p. 132 (see Bibliography for details).

II

influences. With her perennial disorders and frustrated liberties, even a bad coffee crop could produce a revolution, and certainly an economic crisis.[1] She was still a very long way from that democracy which Cecilio Acosta wished she had, namely a democracy which would increase commerce and knowledge of the outside world.

Throughout her history, the geography of Venezuela has exercised a great effect on her people. The extremely poor communications during the latter half of the nineteenth century meant that the territories of the coastal mountains, the llanos and the Andes were isolated and divided from each other. This increased regionalism had made possible the dominance of the local caudillo. The different climates also affected her people. The hot, dry lands were early centres of Spanish colonisation—Coro, Carora and El Tocuyo and the west figuring among these. Caroreños and Corianos were people of the semi-desert. They had to fight against a climate which gave them great physical stamina, stubbornness and resistance. The burning climate under which they lived, the constant struggle which they maintained against the elements and the wild animals, the long journeys which from an early age they had to undertake through the deserted plains, sometimes on foot and sometimes on horseback, gave them an outstanding muscular strength and extraordinary dexterity and agility. The Venezuelan of that region was an offspring of the Spanish, Indian and African races, the connecting link between civilisation and barbarism, between controlling law and liberty without moral restraint; between society with all its conventions and more or less artificial trammels, and the imposing solitude of the desert, where only nature reigns with her immortal grandeur and majesty. The only conqueror these families knew was death,

[1] Report sent by Resident British Minister, Caracas, entitled *Report Upon the Commerce of Venezuela for the Year 1877*, F.O. 199/81. Resident British Minister to Lord Salisbury, Caracas, 20 December 1878, No. 12 Commercial, F.O. 199/83. *Mexican Financier*, 16 July 1887, article 'Venezuela', *South American Journal*, 15 August 1891. Coffee was the keynote of prosperity of the country. When the price of coffee fell, disaster occurred.

which was reflected in their mentality and outlook on life. These people were to become the most famous of Venezuelan soldiers, and the names of the caudillos were like a roll call of the old families: the Rieras, Pereras, Oropesas, to name but a few. They were the sworn enemy to all submission and servility.

The Margariteños were islanders. The sea had made sailors of them, and like most sailors they were quick-witted and versatile. They had a high birth rate and when they worked on the mainland they were much sought after as they were a hard-working people. The hot, slimy lands of the Delta Amacuro had a character all of their own. The people here were strongly influenced by the mighty Orinoco river and they were almost as insular as if they had been on an island, for there are miles and miles of almost impenetrable forest and various channels forming the Delta, the shores covered with walls of reeds and palms so evenly that one might imagine they had been trimmed by the hands of man. The Maracuchos (from Lake Maracaibo) were among the most hardworking and industrious. They were the Catalans of Venezuela. There is little doubt that Lake Maracaibo, with all its tremendous advantages, exercised a great influence on the people, who were very jealous of their rights and whose outlook was distinctly regional. At the end of the nineteenth century, the great international petroleum companies had not yet appeared on the scene, but the Maracuchos were extremely active. They exported all exportable goods, and they were the chief coffee exporters of Venezuela. It was in Maracaibo that the powerful German houses had their headquarters, and throughout this period they were to have a strong influence on the course of events. Maracaibo, the sea-port on Lake Maracaibo, was destined to become an important centre, because it was the natural depôt not only for the western states of Venezuela, but also for the fertile valleys of Cúcuta in Colombia. Lake Maracaibo offered facilities for internal navigation to river craft able to penetrate the interior and bring down to the city produce to be sent to foreign countries. Navigation was not devoid of difficulty in the bar of Maracaibo.

The Andes region was the most remote, but although it did not receive emigrants from abroad, it nevertheless increased its population and also its potential riches. Because of its economical and political aspirations, the Andes was a propitious ground for future caudillos who cashed in on the campesinos' frustrations and unsatisfied dreams. Last but not least there was Caracas,[1] the capital. Caracas was the pride of all Caraqueños who believed it was their god-given right to rule. Despite its pre-eminent position in the country, it remained regional in outlook and all too often it encouraged an aggressive military outlook.

Thus nineteenth century Venezuela, the key to the Caribbean, suffered far too much from regionalism to be ruled easily, and the rulers never tackled the root of the problem, which was economic justice for the masses.

For Venezuelans, the fight for independence had not ended at Ayacucho, it was to be a continual struggle for each succeeding generation. The social spheres were constantly changing: the colonial aristocracy had practically disappeared during the wars of independence,[2] and this was the distinctive difference between her and Colombia, which was still dominated by the aristocratic classes. In Venezuela it had been possible for Paez, one of the people, to rise to the highest post in the land after the wars. Thus Paez had been and remained a symbol of equality. His caudillo's authority was founded on the subconscious suggestion of the majority. To the people Paez represented two aspects of Venezuela which were in themselves paradoxical, the ideal of equality and the dominance of the caudillo. The people felt that through his triumph they themselves ruled Venezuela. Paez's own words on hearing of Bolivar's death expressed their feelings: 'Now *I* am the nation

[1] *South American Journal*, 15 October 1891. An excellent description of Caracas and the life lived there.

[2] Mario Briceño Iragorry, pp. 55–62; and Pedro José Rojas, p. 380—for an English interpretation see R. A. Humphreys, p. 13.

(ahora la patria soy yo)'. Once the Liberator was gone no one could dispute his place as the spiritual representative of the nation. So through him the people's idea of social equality was fulfilled.

Sociologically Venezuela was hardly a country: it was a great revolutionary crowd. There were many armies but no stable army. There was no administration worthy of the name. Venezuela was a formless mass, where superstition and cruelty was predominant—a republic where the years of peace hardly exceeded those of war. From 1830–59 there were eleven armed revolutions, and these constant wars not only exhausted the country physically but also morally, and the passionate hatreds aroused shook the social orders profoundly. The hierarchy of the old Venezuela societies had been founded on revolution and a tradition that militarism was the only co-ordinating force, the instinctive discipline of a stubborn people. Order, when it came, belonged to the bravest caudillo, the most intelligent or the most astute.

Men who knew death habitually were used to non-stop violence; they accepted it as natural. In such a social state the only law they recognised was that of the caudillo. This fulfilled the Venezuelan's idea of equality, for the law thus accepted was that won by their weapons and in this society only the caudillo could be effective for only he could maintain order. It was an unstable social group in the transition stage. The bewilderment that existed made the people turn to the strongest man, and this in the popular mind was the bravest (*mas guapo*) and cleverest. The psychological element was very powerful. What the Venezuelan wanted of his caudillo was a projected image of himself with all the qualities he most admired. To a Venezuelan this meant friendship and force. He wanted him to be decisive and independent, and in return for his obedience he expected absolute protection. The campesino intuitively felt that this all-powerful figure was necessary in this anarchic society.

Because the caudillo loomed so large in Venezuela and

exerted such a tremendous impact on her relations with the outside world, the reasons for caudillism prevailing are important. There are many theories, and as many apologies and explanations as to the necessity for the caudillo. Most Venezuelan historians agree that Venezuela was cursed with this rule of personalism, which contained all the elements of corruption. Inevitably it led to the loss of faith and ideals, as well as to a series of revolutions. But the reason why caudillism flourished has also been interpreted in various ways, and each explanation contains an element of truth. Gil Fortoul has argued that the social condition of the people was largely responsible for their political attitudes. He believed that during the Independence, the fight against the Spaniard had erased the distinction between white, black and Indian, but although after 1830 the coloured (mixed) race predominated, the *social* distinctions persisted. The social and political pre-eminence belonged to an oligarchy of big land-owners and military chiefs. The enormous distances, scanty population coupled with bad communications, meant that there was little commerce and interchange of thought. There was almost a complete lack of education for the people. Under these circumstances, it seemed to Gil Fortoul that caudillism was inevitable.

Another eminent Venezuelan historian, Laureano Vallenilla Lanz, agreed with him up to a point. Vallenilla was the great protagonist of caudillism, but there was a personal reason for this. In order to justify, explain and bolster Gomez's image, his patron and mentor, Vallenilla's brilliant work reiterates the inevitability and necessity of dictatorship in Venezuela. He argued that the war of Independence had meant that the great creole families with all their culture, sensitivity and ideals, had been decimated and had succumbed. The majority of the country therefore was left in a state of savagery (*barbarie*). Once the social barriers had been broken down, the people were no longer restricted, and indulged in orgies of assassination, rape and anarchy. It was the anarchy of all social classes that gave the people the feeling of equality, an idea which was dominant

16

in the history of Venezuela. Independence was won by civil war—Spaniard against Spaniard, Venezuelan against Venezuelan. Men deserted the armies and went to serve under patriot caudillos in favour of the American cause. It was they who supported Paez against the Liberator and attempted to impose the traditional disciplines, those conservative forces of society almost extinguished by the tumultuous democratic movement of the revolution. Paez's prestige was taken advantage of by this realistic colonial element. They encouraged the caudillo Llanero because they thought that under his strong rule he could unify the disruptive forces. Only caudillism could govern.

The reason behind this was that what remained of the creole nobility was ineffective. Patrician families with their ill-digested political theories of the French Revolution constituted the minority which had launched the Independence, and they substituted the prerogatives which had been exercised by the Spaniards for their own. They had grown up in homes where the abuse of prerogatives existed. They now brought to politics those same prejudices which had encouraged revolution and class hatred. The caudillos who emerged were usually from the lower classes and brought forward by a people obsessed with the idea of equality, imposed by ethnic and geographical reasons. To some extent this explains why when the patrician class first gave the cry of independence, the pardos at first opposed them.

According to Vallenilla's theory, the idea of class equality in Venezuela broke out because the equilibrium had been broken by the independence. It was then that ferocious fighting broke out which was unequalled anywhere else in America for its savagery. In turn this barbarism is partly explained by the diverse elements of colonial society. For Vallenilla the dominant race of the caudillos was the logical outcome of the anarchy that had been unleashed. The llaneros could rob and pillage as they had since the early days of the colony. The difference now was that it was hidden under political and constitutional theories. Therefore the ruin and destruction for which they were responsible made it essential for a caudillo to bring back some semblance of order. According to this supposition, caudillos were not a curse but a blessing, for they were men of great character, fully aware of the realities which faced them. They alone were capable of putting an end to those anarchic periods which tore the country apart.

Thus the structure of caudillism in the Venezuela of the nineteenth and early twentieth centuries may be likened to the feudalism in Europe in the Middle Ages. Round the central figure of the caudillo representing the national unity were grouped a number of minor caudillos. These were innumerable individuals who had risen after the Independence when social barriers had disintegrated. They were inspired by their own personal ambitions. Because of them, Venezuela suffered interminable revolutions which nearly always ended with a caudillo imposing his will. These internal convulsions were the manifestations of anarchy, and prelude to a despotic dictatorship. A caudillo could not respect laws which were opposed to what he considered his rights, rights which had been won by force of arms, the conscience of a semi-barbarous people. Vallenilla believed it was a mistake to remove the caudillo, whom he saw as a bulwark against banditry. The only result of trying to substitute political theories for the rule of a caudillo, was a series of wars, e.g. the Federal wars.[1] The interesting point regarding these Venezuelan revolutions is that they were real social revolutions, the result of people's ideas of class equality. This explains the true nature of Venezuelan democracy, which has been the predominance of the individual. It also helps to explain Guzman and Cipriano Castro's dominance, as well as their relations with the great international powers.

If Venezuela's politicians were incapable of coping with her

[1] For further theories, which are essential to the understanding of the Venezuelan people and their relations with Great Britain and other foreigners, see Virgilio Tosta, and for the British point of view see R. A. Humphreys p. 13.

problems except through force, her political thinkers were very active in analysing the country's ills and in formulating political theories. In this way they contributed much to the political life of Venezuela. Just as nations, like individuals, have their crises, these years of transition were also a time of regeneration. The wars that were being waged were really battles between the old and established norms of conduct and the new ways, and in such a society violence and upheaval were natural results. Acosta believed that hope remained, for sometimes life rises from the death of others. His ideas helped to inspire what was best in the country.

It was also accepted that the war of Independence only gave Venezuela independence. It did not give her liberty, for liberty can only come over a long period of time. Liberty is a plant which grows from a seed, it must be developed and have its roots in the life of the nation.

The history of Venezuela from 1830 onwards is the history of its growth. The biggest mistake that Venezuela's rulers made was believing that they could govern without the support of the people. Gonzalez argued that the right to govern does not belong to one person, nor are ideas words that cannot be broken. However, a good government must respect the beliefs of the people, conciliate their interests and take advantage of social forces. He must know how to lead his people. It can only be an anachronism to fight the people. If all these elementary norms were outraged, it seemed to Venezuela's political philosophers that revolution would no longer be an abstract idea. It would spring to life, become a fanatical act, having only one aim, to kill. The importance of these theorists is that they contributed to the political evolution of their country at this particular time in history.

As Venezuela struggled to free itself from one type of society and tried to find another, the various political parties fought to take the lead and seize power. The political parties in Venezuela were the inheritors of the civil wars of independence. The urban population was divided into two groups, the 'godos' and the 'patriotas'. The 'godos' represented commerce, they were the lettered people and the bureaucracy who wished to maintain the colonial regime to protect their interests. They attempted to amplify their prerogatives, which had been almost completely absorbed by the revolutionary mantuanismo. When the wars of independence ended, the 'godos', who above all were realists, saw that the status quo could not be restored, and so they chose as their leader Paez, the all-powerful caudillo, the enemy of the Liberator and of the union with Colombia. The aristocracy that remained was sympathetic towards the Liberals, upholding the economic doctrines of the liberal school of Manchester, and was greatly influenced by British political thought.

The year 1840 is important in that it marks the official founding of the Liberal party. At that time it lacked a well-developed political philosophy, even though it was influenced by European (mainly British) thought. The man who was to develop his socialist ideas and adapt them to Venezuela's problems was Tomas Lander, even though the great protagonist in the press was Antonio Leocadio Guzman, father of Antonio Guzman Blanco. Each party fought to dominate the country, but neither attempted to cope with the root of Venezuela's problems which was her economy. Theirs was a policy of opportunism. The key to much of Venezuela's nineteenth-century history lies in this power struggle of expediency between the two political parties. And it was the manner in which this political power was transferred from the mantuanos (oligarchs) to the Liberals, which led to the rise of Antonio Guzman Blanco and Cipriano Castro. This affected not only Venezuela's domestic policy but also her relations with Great Britain and the other great powers.

The long years of the Monagas rule had far-reaching results.[1] In the domestic field, hardly a day passed without someone being persecuted. There were countless risings against the Monagas; all were crushed ruthlessly by their lancers from

[1] The long years were: 1847–51, José Tadeo Monagas; 1851–5, José Gregorio Monagas; 1855–8 José Tadeo Monagas.

Oriente. This in turn encouraged the rise of regionalism and augmented the jealousies between the regions themselves. The administrative incapacity of the Monagas Governments, the low morality of the Monagas brothers, who surrounded themselves with men devoid of all principles, produced a profound economic malaise, which was aggravated by pests, epidemics, hunger, etc. Venezuela swung between tumultuous anarchy and despotic order. Belford Wilson, the Resident British Minister in Caracas, was well aware of the corruption and dishonesty of the Monagas regime. He knew too well that they were plotting to establish their 'dynasty', for it was an unquestionable fact that the first Monagas and his partisans organised a 'revolution' and then set aside the election of any other but a Monagas, i.e. José Gregorio Monagas. As the election was the result of corruption, fraud and coercion, there was little prospect that the nation would patriotically and honestly collaborate with the President in promoting the prosperity of the country.

Already, as early as this, the seeds of future trouble regarding Great Britain's relations with Venezuela were being sown. The feeling of country and congress was definitely hostile towards foreigners. Wilson was well aware of the inherent dangers should British subjects interfere in the domestic politics of the country. The principle of non-intervention was generally upheld by the British Legation, an attitude which was warmly approved of by the Foreign Office. One of the main sources of grievance of British subjects in Venezuela was that they rarely received redress in Venezuelan courts. This was often due to the malpractices of the Venezuelan courts, very often to the character of the judges who themselves were responsible for miscarriages of justice. With rare exceptions, the judges were violent political partisans. They were elected and appointed because of their extreme views and services to the dominant faction of the day, rather than with regard to their personal character or respect for legal qualifications. Under these cir cumstances there was very often little chance of foreigners obtaining redress. This question involved the security of British subjects, property and safety of commercial transactions. It was a curious fact that the Monagas family saw the dangers inherent in this, and were extremely well disposed towards Wilson. Yet their opponents tried to bring on a collision between the two countries in order to overthrow them. In so doing they demonstrated the parochialness and lack of vision in international affairs which was to be one of the causes of the Anglo-German blockade.

Not only were the Liberals striving to overthrow the Monagas family but the patricians were also facing one of their biggest dilemmas. They wanted to seize and wield power but they were not prepared to accept the responsibility of being President. They needed a puppet leader who would do their bidding. This was their inherent weakness, and it was to be their downfall. The representative of the old creole nobility was Manuel Felipe de Tovar, a prominent conservative. His friend, kinsman and adviser was Fermin Toro. In Venezuelan history, Fermin Toro remains one of the great political figures representing the love of liberty and human dignity in civic life. This too was his weakness, for he was far in advance of his time. Similarly, Tovar did not belong to the world in which he lived. At that particular point in history, it would have been easy for Manuel Tovar to have become the caudillo, the country's leader, but this was not in his tradition, nor was it what he had been taught. His attitude was outmoded and paternalistic. He was too aristocratic and sensitive. Because he had spent many years in Europe and was imbued with European culture, he was ill-equipped to deal with the problems of a very underdeveloped country. Tovar was completely out of touch with the ordinary Venezuelan, for he was unable to grasp the effects which an all-embracing poverty had on the lower and rural classes. It turned the men of the llanos into ferocious beasts, semi-pariahs. The law had given them their freedom but it had failed to give them the means of subsistence. History now demanded a new caudillo in order to replace the Monagas family. Erroneously, Tovar and Toro believed that the union of parties and country could only be achieved through a military leader. They felt that the new caudillo should not belong to the old hierarchy of criollans (creoles), the conservative oligarchy. Nor did it seem worth while to replace the personalism of the Monagas with the anachronistic one of Paez. But they could not win because they were trying to fight the same evil which was triumphant everywhere in Venezuela, i.e. Monaguismo, the same thing as caudillism and which was later to become Guzmanismo, or autocratic rule. Tovar and Toro committed the cardinal error of finding a weak and traitorous leader for their revolution, namely Julian Castro. This was because through him they believed that they would be able to govern democratically, at any rate to some extent. They also expected the two parties, Conservative and Liberal, would be represented and united in the Government, thus establishing it on a 'national' basis. In this way the March Revolution which overthrew Monagas would be exempt from the cult of personalism.

In the beginning, the fact that Julian Castro was such an undistinguished soldier and politician contributed to the alliance of Conservative and Liberals. But once the initial enthusiasm waned, Castro's indifferent talents, instead of remaining the uniting factor, became his great weakness. Suspicions and quarrels arose, and Castro himself, who had never been noted for his loyalty, attempted to play one party against the other in the belief that he could form a party of his own from the various discontented factions. He only succeeded in precipitating his own downfall, plunging the country into the bloodiest of civil wars. Not only was his failure directly responsible for the devastating Federal wars, but it helped to entrench the caudillos in power, and marked a further step in Guzman Blanco's rise to power.

The March Revolution was marked by three stages. The first stage embraced the preliminaries leading up to the revolution itself, to be followed rapidly by the three main problems facing the revolutionaries. These were: what to do with the deposed Monagas; the intervention of foreign powers in his defence; and the threat of armed force with the appearance of men-of-war ships at La Guaira. These events were to affect Venezuela's relations with Great Britain and the great powers. The threat to the nation's sovereignty was as a prelude to the later Anglo-German blockade in 1902–3.[1] The second stage was characterised by Castro's vacillations and intrigues, as well as by Paez's manoeuvrings to seize power. As a background to the main events which were played out in Caracas, the Federal wars broke out all over the country. The death and anarchy which were unleashed were like a Greek chorus to the nation's tragedy. When the wars finally ended, one figure had emerged supreme as the future leader—Guzman Blanco, although the nominal leader was the good natured, gentle Falcon. The future lay with Guzman Blanco, and it was he who was to initiate that despotic caudillism which was to torture Venezuela from 1870 to 1935.

[1] The show of force was ever present in the minds of the great powers when they wished to impose their rights and ideas. Belford Wilson—Palmerston, 5 March 1851, No. 21, F.O. 200/26. Wilson requests Dundonald to send Captain Cochrane to La Guaira. It was an unquestionable fact that in the throes of a crisis, a show of force, i.e. 'gunboat diplomacy', was all too often used by the great powers for the purpose of intimidation.

Chapter 2

Venezuela: the Second Half of the Nineteenth Century

While President Monagas was preparing to establish his dynasty even more firmly, the Liberals and Conservatives were searching for a leader who would unite them. Above all they sought someone who would be exempt from the cult of personalism. Their only choice was one of Monagas' lieutenants, namely Julian Castro. Besides the problem of choosing a leader, there was the financial aspect. As early as 1856–7, Paez was writing from New York that he wished to lead their revolution, but that he needed money. Tovar and Toro were able to emphasise the monetary difficulties in order to gain time while they found a more acceptable leader. This was not too difficult as many of the other revolutionaries found Paez unfavourable. Indeed, an amusing story is told of a prominent liberal who even suggested that Monagas should be given 1 million pesos per annum to deter him from robbing the nation, for if the pecuniary temptation were removed, he would then make a very good ruler. The fact that Paez was passed over in favour of a nonentity was something he never forgot nor forgave. Meanwhile, in order to finance the revolution, Tovar offered his own fortune, thereby becoming responsible for providing both the leader and the money.

The revolution proper broke out in March 1858 and this marked the beginning of the second stage. On 15 March 1858 Monagas realised he had lost, and resigned the presidency. He presented his resignation in generous enough terms, which were accepted by Congress. The important point was that at this phase the revolution had been short and comparatively blood-less. Three prominent figures remained at the head of the Government: Julian Castro, so-called leader, Tovar the power behind the throne, wielding the power for which he had striven, and Toro, his adviser, kinsman and friend. The preparations were over. Julian Castro's weaknesses and vacillations were now to be responsible for the revolutionaries' immediate difficulties.

Julian Castro did not realise that he headed this revolution not because he was a born caudillo, but because he was incapable of rousing passions as Paez might have done, and above all because he was unimportant. He was completely dependent on both the Liberal and the Conservative parties, and had few original ideas of his own. He took advice from both but his judgement was weak, with unfortunate results for his administration and country. Anxious to conciliate all those whom he could, he demanded monetary reparation from those officers who had been in charge of public funds and who had failed to render a satisfactory account. It was well nigh impossible to force people to return land or money. The only concrete result arising from his demands was that he filled his followers with fear and distrust. The other measure which Castro took, and which had far-reaching results, concerned his dealings with Monagas himself. The Monagas family had always endeavoured to keep good relations between themselves and the Resident British Minister and had done their best to avoid a clash between Venezuela and the great powers. Monagas now profited from this and took refuge in the French Embassy when the revolutionary army entered Caracas. Urrutia, Castro's Minister for Foreign Affairs, decided in conjunction with the diplomatic corps, but without consulting his own colleagues, that Monagas should be detained in his own house in Caracas, and that no action should be taken against him. As Urrutia's colleagues saw it, the diplomatic corps was being allowed to exert moral pressure on what should have been a domestic issue. Consequently the Venezuelan Government considered this a dangerous precedent, for the sovereignty of the nation was at stake if the diplomatic corps' action was accepted. The situation was further aggravated by the British and French Legations' claims that their residences had been attacked by the mob as an act of vengeance. They demanded reparation. On 8 May, British and French men-of-war entered La Guaira harbour and requested peremptorily that the Venezuelan Government should apologise. They also stated that they expected the safety of Monagas to be assured.

The Venezuelans denied that the Legations had been attacked, and Toro stated that under no circumstances could Venezuela accept the intervention of foreign powers in the domestic affairs of Venezuela. Yet a dangerous precedent had been set which augured ill for the future. The immediate result was the resignation of the Foreign Minister, Urrutia, a Liberal. The Conservative party were now predominant in the Government. As the revolution had come about because of the delicate balance which had been struck between the two parties, the Liberals felt they were being ousted. Juan Crisóstomo Falcon and his son-in-law Ezequiel Zamora, both prominent Liberals, found they were being pushed aside and consequently fled to the West Indies to prepare for a new revolution. Their departure was to herald the beginning of the bloody Federal wars which lasted from 1859–70.[1]

Meanwhile, because a small but active group of counter-revolutionaries tried to overthrow Julian Castro even before the presidential elections could take place, he exiled a vast number of Liberals. Among those who fell victim were Antonio Leocadio Guzman[2] and his son Antonio Guzman Blanco. Both were conspicuous Liberals. The fact that father and son were

---

[1] R. A. Humphreys, p. 13: 'But for many years, and over large parts of Spanish America, it was the law of force, not the force of law that held most governments in power and since force could only be met by force, revolution became an essential element in the political system.'

[2] Belford Wilson—Palmerston, undated, partly torn, F.O. 200/26: 'Antonio Leocadio Guzman, principal leader of the opposition, who had first braved the

exiled at this point marks another significant step in Antonio Guzman Blanco's rise to power. His father, the older man, chose to follow the younger, more tempestuous exiled leader, that is to say Zamora, in the belief that it would be Zamora who would eventually seize power. His son, younger but nevertheless more astute and far-seeing, would nail his colours to the mast of the gentler, older man's banner, Falcon. As his able and trusted lieutenant, Guzman would use his position of trust with Falcon, in order to seize power for himself.

Antonio Leocadio Guzman's main importance lies in the fact that he was Antonio Guzman's father. As such, it is interesting to note what influence, if any, he had on his son and on his son's rise to power. The older man, a strong, ambitious figure, appears insignificant beside that of his more famous son. Like his son, the father was unscrupulous, and desired above all to rise to the highest posts of the republic. But it was his destiny never to attain his ambition and ever to play the role of second fiddle. He attacked the patricians because he was unable to break down the barriers which separated him from them. He was underhand and devious and tried to be all things to all men. A popular political paper described him as brave with the defeated, gentle with the victors, and subservient to every cause. He served the Monarchy against the Republic, Paez against Bolivar, Monagas against Paez, and at that particular time, the revolution against Monagas, followed by another revolution against Julian Castro whom he had previously supported. He was the perfect criollan 'Vicar of Bray'. But he had one great asset. He was able to promote the cause of the lower classes, the campesinos, by putting into ordinary language the great liberal ideas which were helping to mould the new Europe. No one proclaimed liberal philosophy more vociferously than did Leocadio Guzman. Unfortunately, these

power of the oligarchy, denounced oppression and abuses . . . man of ability and information, freer than most from prejudices against foreigners.'

ideas and ideals were always sacrificed to his one great ambition which was the attainment of power. Though his life was a dismal failure, by his articles and speeches he was able to rouse a few consciences. He remained what he was, a little man with big ideas, but his political manoeuvrings taught his son, Antonio Guzman, the art of expediency and opportunism.

By the very act of exiling his enemies, Julian Castro set the ball in motion and handed over the initiative to his enemies so that they could organise a counter-revolution against him. It was also to be the decisive step in Guzman Blanco's rise to power, and it was to mark the beginning of the third stage of the March Revolution. Castro had left himself with no alternative but to form his government from the Conservative party only. These were now called Godos, oligarchs or centralists, and curiously enough they would fight under the red flag. The opposition now openly consisted of the Liberal party for all pretence at unity had collapsed. As their chief ideal, they put forward the principal of Federation, in opposition to a centralised form of government. But if the leaders knew what they were seeking (which was political power), the people did not —they naively believed that Federation would cure all their ills, and were so confused as to the true meaning of the word 'federal', that they even mispronounced it as 'feberal'. This vagueness enabled Guzman Blanco to do more or less what he wished with the people.

On 15 October, at San Tomas, a patriotic junta of Venezuela was instituted. The junta's chief aim was to try and obtain an independent administrative system of the provinces based on the federal pattern, with more liberal ideas of government prevailing. A few months later, from Palma Sola, Falcon launched a proclamation. He declared that instead of passing a number of new laws, it was far more important for Venezuela that she should enjoy the freedom which was essential if free elections were to take place. After free elections, a more constitutional form of government could be formed. As far as Falcon himself was concerned, this was to be the main objective of the counter-revolution. But hardly any of the other leaders believed in the principle of federation. At the congress of 1867, A. L. Guzman cynically declared that he could not understand why the Venezuelan people were so enamoured with the idea of federation, since he was certain they did not understand its real meaning. The idea had been created by himself and others because they knew that all revolutions needed a banner under which to fight, and this had served the purpose admirably. Moreover, the convention of Valencia (Julian Castro's) had not called their constitution federal. This had automatically allowed them to use the word as a rallying cry for the people. Any other would have served equally well.

This cynicism illustrated that A. L. Guzman, as well as the other revolutionary leaders, was incapable of understanding the aspirations of the Venezuelan people. For them the revolution remained a genuine social one. It was not merely a political manoeuvre by which two parties seized power. It was more than that. It represented a nation's hope. They truly believed it would lead to the attainment of social equality, and so cure all their social ills. Like all primitive people, they became obsessed with the power they thought that one word represented, a magic future!

Meanwhile the country was being devastated by numerous uprisings, and Julian Castro's weakness was becoming more and more apparent. At one stage he attempted to throw the onus of government on Tovar, who had been elected vice-president. By retiring temporarily on the pretext of ill-health, Castro forced Tovar to take difficult and unpopular decisions. Then, for no apparent reason, Castro decided to govern once more, leaving Tovar high and dry. Paez, who had been recalled from exile, added to the confusion by his unscrupulous intriguing. In order to improve his prospects, he decided to leave the country, giving his followers even more of an incentive. Castro now became quite incapable of governing or of imposing his will, and made overtures to the Liberals. Before he could betray his own Government to the revolutionaries, they imprisoned him, so great was their distrust of his duplicity. In this way Castro found himself hoist with his own petard, for Liberals and Conservatives united in overthrowing him.

The third and final stage of the March Revolution was completed with the brief period of Tovar's presidency. In 1860, Congress proclaimed Tovar President and Pedro Gual Vice-president. Tovar's was an undistinguished Government. Its main preoccupation was the defeat of the revolution led by Falcon and Zamora. Even the fact that Tovar set Castro free and exiled him was a negative measure, for in fact Castro did not endanger the Government's stability.

If these years in Venezuela's history are administratively undistinguished, they are outstanding for their violence. The Federal revolutionaries, less well armed than the Government forces, knew that it was to their advantage to prolong the war, wage guerrilla warfare, and initiate as many uprisings as possible. Two results emerged from this chaos. Tovar took every possible measure to ruthlessly crush the revolution. The far-reaching result was the emergence of Antonio Guzman Blanco.[1] He was Falcon's most outstanding lieutenant with the death of his chief rival, Ezequiel Zamora.[2] Zamora is one of those leaders whom death robbed of a glorious future. He was the great leader of the Federal wars, and he possessed the quality of leadership to an outstanding degree. His men worshipped him, and as he achieved one military victory after another, it seemed as if the nation's destiny would be in his hands. Once Falcon joined forces with Zamora there was no question of Falcon, or even Guzman, directing a military operation.

The military genius was Zamora, and Guzman Blanco fully realised Zamora's outstanding talents. In 1860, a bullet was fired by an unknown enemy and Zamora was killed. The man who was with him at the time was Guzman Blanco himself, and

---

[1] *Star and Herald*, 13 March 1879, article *Venezuela's Great Soldier*.

[2] Laureano Vallenilla Lanz: *Vida del Valiente Ciudadano General Ezequiel Zamora*, Caracas, 1898. Diaz-Sanchez, pp. 442–52, note 641 particularly interesting.

with Zamora's death, he was the only remarkable figure left among Falcon's men.

Thus Zamora's death marked a decisive step in Guzman's career.

When Zamora's death became known, panic spread through the Federal forces; after a series of military defeats, Falcon, accompanied by his secretary Guzman Blanco, fled to Colombia. In Venezuela, anarchy continued. But if the country was split and up in arms, Tovar's Government was equally divided. Tovar headed the faction which advocated strong measures against the Federalist menace. His opponents were led by Paez's able lieutenant and friend, Pedro José Rojas. As a solution, he advised a 'dictatorship'. He worked unceasingly towards this end. Perhaps because of his innate honesty, Tovar refused to believe that he was being betrayed and that his Government was in danger.

In March 1860, Paez returned to Venezuela from New York recalled by the advocates of the dictatorship. Tovar sought to counter-act and appointed Paez as head of the Army, but by so doing he fanned even further the old caudillo's ambitions. From then on Tovar's administration was plagued by political manoeuvrings until his government was completely undermined. This was Paez's revenge for not having been chosen leader of the March Revolution. By 20 May, Tovar realised he could no longer govern and he resigned, marking the end of the mantuano rule. One of the most able descriptions of the rule of the mantuanos was that of Juan Vicente Gonzalez.[1] Tovar was too aristocratic, too out of touch with the ordinary Venezuelan of his time, to be able to govern successfully. His people distrusted him because they could not understand him, for they were invariably on a different wavelength. Finally, he lacked the ruthlessness which was to distinguish Guzman Blanco and the other caudillos who followed him.[2]

[1] Juan Vicente Gonzalez, p. 311.
[2] See also Gil Fortoul, p. 187. In 1888, Tovar died in Paris, a voluntary exile.

The departure of Tovar left the door wide open for Paez. For a few short weeks, Gual, the Vice-president, attempted to stem the tide which was flowing in Paez's favour. But Gual was already an old man of seventy-seven, and more suited to rule in peace time. By the end of August the constitutional party was dead and Gual had fled into exile. The appalling condition of the country had contributed to this state of affairs. Gual's departure marked the end of the March Revolution and the beginning of Paez's dictatorship. Ultimately, the real reason why Paez triumphed was the state in which Venezuela found herself. The wars had undermined the nation and left it exhausted. The people longed to be governed, and to have a caudillo who would curtail the power and tyranny of capital. The upper classes wanted money to build railways, which would help communications and commerce, and bring money into the country.

Everyone agreed they needed peace and they believed Paez was the one person who could give it them. Moreover, the constitutional party had died because of internal dissensions and those who could have defended it had fled. Later on, the people's dream was broken by the reality of the dictatorship, and this augmented their tragedy. The great protagonist Juan Vicente Gonzalez realised this, and he spoke for the country when he wrote that Paez had destroyed the legend which the love and admiration for him had created.

When Paez seized power, he did not appoint a proper ministry, since Pedro José Rojas, whom Tovar had feared so much, was all things to all men and represented all the ministries. The administration *in toto* was in his hands. There were no elections. Instead Paez preferred to meet Falcon. This meeting failed to produce any concrete results because of Paez's exorbitant demands, and the distrust which he aroused in the Federalists. Falcon's proposals were reasonable and should have been accepted. These were: that hostilities should cease; that a provisional government should be presided over by Paez with a coalition government; that a constituent assembly should meet and both parties be represented. It was also proposed that the provisional Government should resign before the Assembly, and that the Assembly should appoint new governors until the new constitution was promulgated. Finally, Falcon was to remain head of the Federal army which would encamp in a prearranged place. Other attempts to come to an understanding were then made, the most important being one wherein there was a meeting which Falcon did not attend personally, but instead sent his friend and representative Antonio Guzman Blanco. Though the negotiations broke down, it marked a further step in Guzman's rise to power. Armed conflict continued, anarchy reigned everywhere, but Falcon remained in his own province. There was little doubt that Falcon's weakness was a decisive factor in Guzman's career, for Falcon could not cope with the activities of war in the energetic way that Guzman could.

At last Falcon was compelled to move. He was no military genius but he had the inestimable gift of choosing the right man for the right place. First it had been Zamora, and death had robbed him of victory. Then another rival of Guzman's, Urdaneta, had also been killed. Falcon now chose and sent Guzman to direct military operations. Guzman himself had no doubts concerning his military prowess[1] and his military flair stood him in good stead, for he was able to seize the initiative and win. Instead of seeking pitched battles, he organised guerrilla warfare and wherever he could he conciliated the small caudillos and won them over to Falcon's cause.[2] Guzman wielded one of the best weapons of the war: the ideals were held by the Liberals and Guzman exploited this to the full.[3] He preached far and wide the equality of class, and made the people

[1] According to his modest estimate Venezuela may be congratulated on the possession of the most celebrated military chieftain which the world has ever seen. See *Cosmopolitan*, 27 March 1873.

[2] Guzman Blanco had an excellent opinion of himself as a military man—*Star and Herald*, 13 March 1879: 'Venezuela's Great Soldier'—'As a commanding general I have no rival in America nor here even in Europe'.

[3] See Gil Fortoul, p. 203. See also Diaz-Sanchez, p. 438.

believe that this equality could be attained by federation. In the long term, the Federal wars broke down the barriers between the social classes completely, and achieved racial integration. In the short term, Guzman skilfully manipulated the people's desire for social equality to seek his own ends, and become the 'soul and inspiration' of the revolution. He was convinced that most men had their price, and that what most seek is money.[1] His friend Rojas[2] also had illusions regarding the importance of finance and negotiation. This was the main reason why he sent Nadal to London to try and obtain a loan.[3]

Rojas attempted to negotiate a peace treaty with Guzman Blanco, but it was Venezuela's tragedy that the negotiations broke down and the armed conflict continued.

---

[1] As was Gomez later on. Money was the mainspring of Gomez's power as it was of Guzman's.

[2] Pedro José Rojas, Paez's friend and adviser. He was a 'friend' of Guzman also.

[3] H. Nadal—Doveton Orme, 22 November 1861, F.O. 80/164. *The Times*, 2 April 1862, p. 10 Letter from Hilarion Nadal, Paez's fiscal agent, setting out the objects of his mission, chief of which was to 'enable Paez to complete the pacification of the country so successful up till now, and in which foreign and internal creditors are so deeply interested.'

Chapter 3

❧❧

Venezuela's Debt: the 1862 Loan and its Repercussions

'British merchants and manufacturers, British capitalists, in
short, the whole British publick, are eagerly turning their
eyes . . . to the American hemisphere. They are endeavour-
ing to link Britain to these new states, by every tie that excited
cupidity can devise, and enormous opulence carry into effect.
Nothing was ever like it before. . . .' R. A. Humphreys,
p. 149.

See W. R. Manning and J. F. Rippy, 1959.

'The Spanish Republics provided an obvious outlet for Victorian
Britain's surplus capital, and the figure of £23 million worth of
the produce and manufactures of Great Britain, exported to
Latin America in 1900—£3 million more than the total British
exports to the United States—provides an indication of the
manufacturing interests at stake. Latin America, throughout
the nineteenth century, supplied an invaluable market for
British goods, which at first commanded a virtual monopoly.'[1]
For this, as well as for historical reasons, it seemed to the young
Spanish republics perfectly natural to turn to the London market
in order to obtain loans.[2] Despite the fact that Venezuela did

[1] D. C. M. Platt, p. 3.
[2] Edward B. Eastwick, p. 230, 'Venezuela owes England a very great deal
for her help in the wars of independence'. See also: Committee of Spanish
American Bondholders, Mr Powles—Captain Mathews, London, 9 June 1864.

not keep faith with her bondholders, either from want of revenue, through troubles of internal war or similar causes, nevertheless loans continued to be granted, for the London capitalists felt that there remained a wide scope for remunerative and successful enterprises even in defaulting Venezuela.

Paez and Rojas were faced with what amounted to almost insuperable economic problems. The young republic had inherited many of these because of the wars of independence, for in order to wage war, she had been forced to contract loans over the years, and these had become a source of much trouble. In order to realise the role which the Venezuelan debt had on her relations with Great Britain, and indeed on her domestic policy, a brief account is necessary. The history of the Venezuelan debt is inseparably mixed up with that of Colombia and Ecuador, the three countries at the time of the Independence forming the republic of Colombia. The War of Independence was the cause of the debt, contracted under unfavourable circumstances, and increased by the arrears of interest upon interest during the long years of internal disturbances which followed the war against Spain.[1]

The first steps towards the formation of this debt were taken by Real Mendez, and Lopez Mendez, the former as Representative of New Granada, and the latter as agent for Venezuela in London, who entered into several contracts for the delivery of war materials, the engagement and pay of about 5,080 soldiers and officers from Britain to aid the new countries in their war of emancipation. Britain must have helped from egotistical motives. Nevertheless it is noteworthy that no Englishman was known to have enlisted under the Spanish flag of despotism.

P.R.O. F.O. 80/176: 'My sense of the value of the help which you and other Englishmen similarly interested rendered to the young republic at the time when it was much wanted.'

[1] Committee of Venezuelan Bondholders—Earl of Clarendon, 13 January 1866, P.R.O. F.O. 80/184. An account of the Debt. See also E. B. Eastwick, *op. cit.*

When Colombia was constituted in 1819, Bolivar sent to Europe Vice-President Zea, with full powers and instructions for the establishment of diplomatic relations, and for negotiating a loan. At the time of Zea's arrival in London, the debt of the Colombian republic principally contracted, as already said, for the purposes of war, clothing of soldiers, etc., amounted to only about $2,500,000, i.e. £500,000. In order to re-establish the credit of Colombia, Zea called together the creditors, represented by Messrs Herring, Graham and Powels, and entered into an agreement with them on 1 August 1820, in which he recognised a debt of $3,658,810. A supplementary agreement was afterwards entered into for the settlement of claims to the extent of $919,890, making a total of $4,578,700 or about £915,750. By these unfortunate contracts, the debt of Colombia was increased by £415,750; and he issued debentures bearing 10 per cent interest if paid in Britain and 12 per cent if paid in Colombia, in settlement thereof.

In February 1821, in spite of the fact that Zea was the only authorised agent of Colombia in Europe, Lopez Mendez entered into a contract with J. Mackintosh for the supply of equipment and armaments for $10,000; $75 (£15) being paid for rifle and clothing of every soldier, and interest at the rate of 10 per cent. He issued debenture bonds to the extent of $750,000 for these purposes. When the interest on these debentures fell due, and no funds were forthcoming for their payment, Zea, desirous of raising a further sum of money, contracted another loan with Messrs Herring, Graham and Powels for $700,000. This loan was sold at 65 per cent, and with the proceeds thereof the overdue interest was met. Subsequently, in March 1822, Zea arranged with the same firm for a 6 per cent loan of $10,000,000 at 80 per cent, 2 per cent issue commission being allowed. The principal objects of this new transaction were the amortisation of the former debentures and the acquisition of additional war material and clothing for the soldiers. In 1823, the Congress of Colombia repudiated this onerous transaction on account of the fact that Zea had no authority at the time of the signature of the contract with Messrs Herring, Graham and Powels, to compromise the revenue of the country. Later on, they were forced to recognise the debt.

In July 1823, the Congress of Colombia authorised the Government to contract an internal or external loan for £6,000,000, and on 1 April 1824 an agreement was reached with the former financiers, whereby all the claims against the Colombian republic were recognised. The financiers returned $875,000, a balance which they confessed was due to Colombia, out of $10,000,000 contracted for by Zea. After this arrangement, which disposed of $10,000,000, the balance of the authorised 6 per cent loan, i.e. $20,000,000, was placed with Messrs B. A. Goldschmidt & Co., at 85 per cent. This latter contract was signed in London on 22 April 1824, but a portion of the bonds was signed at Calais and the balance at Hamburg, owing to some difficulties as to the rate of interest. The total amount of debt stood then at £6,750,000, each dollar being taken at 4s 6d.

With the moneys received from this loan, an expedition of 4,000 men was sent by Colombia to Peru, and this absorbed a great portion of the funds available. In 1826, Goldschmidt & Co. failed, and their failure caused Colombia a loss of $2,010,995.75, or say in round figures, £500,000. When, in 1830, the Republic of Colombia was dissolved,[1] and Venezuela and Ecuador became independent states, it became necessary to settle the proportion of the debt appertaining to each of the new and separate republics. In December 1834, the commissioners of Venezuela and New Granada, after waiting in vain during many months for the Ecuador commissioner, signed a convention at Bogota, with reference to the division of the debt. The basis thereof was taken to be the population of the three republics according to the census of 1825. Upon this basis, New Granada became liable for 50 per cent, Venezuela for 18½ per cent (total £2,794,826; no interest was paid by Vene-

[1] 22 September 1830, Congreso Constituyente en Valencia.

zuela until 1841), and Ecuador 21½ per cent. This convention was ratified by Venezuela in 1835, by Ecuador and New Granada in 1837; but it was not until 16 May 1839 that a final settlement was reached.[1]

Up to 1830, the material prosperity of Venezuela had grown, but from 1840–4 exports fell drastically, and consequently imports were also reduced. As the customs duties constituted one of the mainstays of the Government's source of income, this led to a deterioration of the economy, which was probably due to a decrease in the nation's rent, a result of the laws governing exports by which duties were reduced considerably and finally suppressed.

There were other reasons why the economic crisis grew worse at this particular period. The Government was accused of having contributed to this situation because of a concession granted to the Banco Nacional and the fact that the nation's income was used to buy the bank's shares. The opposition attacked the Government and accused it of using the nation's money to found the bank when this could have been done with private capital. According to the Liberals, the country's economic difficulties were increased by the policy of the Conservatives. The Conservatives in their turn accused the Venezuelan coffee growers of not foreseeing the international crisis regarding the price of coffee. Because of this, they jeopardised their estates and exacerbated the social conditions.

In order to endeavour to arrive at a settlement with the foreign bondholders for the 28½ per cent of the Colombian debt which Venezuela had taken over, Alejo Fortique was despatched to London by the Venezuelan Government. For a country of only 1 million inhabitants, as Venezuela then was, it was not a small sum. On 16 September 1840, the Government of Venezuela issued a decree with reference to their proportion

---

[1] *Council of Foreign Bondholders*, 16th Annual Report. Belford Hinton Wilson—Joshua Schofield, Caracas, 1 January 1884, P.R.O. F.O. 80/183. Daniel O'Leary and Josébi Plata—Memorial Relating to Debt, Bogota, 26 January 1854, P.R.O. F.O. 80/183.

of the debt, and this was accepted by the Colombian bond-holders. The conversion of these bonds for new Venezuelan securities was at once proceeded with and the amount thereof was £3,276,791.10 or $23,604,942.12, at $6.25 per pound. The importance of this decree was that this pact was between the British bondholders of the Colombian debt and the Venezuelan Government. It was a triumph for both parties, since they transferred the problem from the international sphere to a private one: the contracts were now between the Venezuelan Government and private individuals. This is very significant as the debt could no longer be considered diplomatic. It was an aspect of some consequence during the Anglo-German block-ade of 1902-3 and after.

Under the administration of General Carlos Soublette, the interest on the debt was paid, but the situation changed under the two Monagas, 1847-58.

Under the administration of General José Tadeo Monagas, the interest was paid on 1 April 1847 with funds deposited with the Venezuelan agents in London, Reid Irving & Co.—this was the last regular payment. Reid Irving & Co. went bankrupt and unexpectedly suspended payments, thus jeopardising the funds which they held from the Government. It was impossible for the Venezuelan Government to pay the interest when it became due. Later on, the fact that the firm went bankrupt was given many times as an excuse for the non-existence of Venezuela's credit abroad. The truth of the matter was that the firm was only responsible for the republic losing £18,693.11.8d, which should have merely caused a delay in the payment of interest. The expenses of the war were privately admitted by the Government as being the real reason for the continued non-payment of interest, and not the bankruptcy of the firm. From April 1847-54, no interest was paid, and by 1858, when the rule of the Monagas came to an end, the external debt had increased by $4,956,783.66 over and above $20,962.87 which was owed. Abroad, Venezuela's credit was completely non-existent. The bondholders felt that 'the object of the Venezuelan Finance

Minister is to procrastinate—to avoid as long as possible coming to an arrangement'. They were thoroughly convinced that unless H.M.'s Government intervened authoritatively, the bondholders would ultimately have to succumb.

'The bondholders found their richest source for diplomatic intervention, naturally enough, in the British Government, but the British Government remained traditionally reluctant to intervene by force of arms.' H.M.'s Government attempted a policy of neutrality as regards the Venezuelan Government's debts and the predicaments in which the Council of Foreign Bondholders all too often found themselves. At the same time there is little doubt that officially the policy of the Foreign Office was restricted to 'referring to the principles laid down in Lord Palmerston's despatch of 18 March 1831 . . . to the simple exercise of good offices. . . .' However, there appears to be a slight divergence of emphasis in the attitude adopted by the Foreign Office in London, and the diplomats who were in Venezuela. The latter pressed the claims of the Council of Foreign Bondholders with more vigour than the strictly official view suggested. The Foreign Office view tended to be sympathetic towards the Venezuelan Government's financial difficulties which did 'not warrant intervention by H.M.'s Government'. After repeated requests from the bondholders and Baring & Co., the only concession which the Foreign Office made was to name the British Consul in Venezuela as their agent for the collection of dues for payment of bondholders. The Foreign Office also allowed the British Consul General in Venezuela to act, for a limited period, as Baring's agent or representative, for the purpose of forwarding to them the portion of the custom's receipts which were to be pledged by the Venezuelan Government to the British bondholders. This consent was only temporary, and with the clear understanding that it was a private arrangement, i.e. one between the consul and Baring. In no way was H.M.'s Government responsible for anything connected either with the receipt or transmission of the funds in question. This policy was reinforced by

Foreign Office instructions to Doveton-Orme, the Resident British Minister in Caracas. Doveton-Orme was instructed to act as Baring's representative 'but strictly to observe conditions'. Baring Brothers wrote to Layward, the Under Secretary of State for Foreign Affairs, thanking the Foreign Office for the concession 'although it was not as full as we had hoped but will be of aid'.

The Foreign Office attitude was invariably as non-commital as possible since they were frightened of becoming involved in private transactions which could lead them to undesirable disputes with the Venezuelan Government. The attitude of private capitalists and foreign bondholders was to try and obtain as much official backing as they could from both the Foreign Office and H.M.'s legation in Caracas. They were well aware that even such an arrangement as that to which the Foreign Office had reluctantly consented, would carry considerable weight with the Venezuelan Government, who would certainly find it difficult to distinguish between 'an official and private capacity' since the Consul General was the 'official' representative of H.M.'s Government. The arguments which the Foreign Office might put forward seemed to them to beg the question. Herein lay the future danger for both governments. The danger, as far as Venezuela was concerned, was exacerbated by the extreme poverty of the country, and its appalling state. With the advent to power of General J. A. Paez, Dictator of Venezuela, on the whole much admired in Great Britain, Venezuela felt the time was ripe to seek a new loan from London. Accordingly, Hilarion Nadal, Paez's fiscal agent, tried to explain the Government's situation to Doveton-Orme. The duty of the Government was to defend itself, he wrote, and he realised that payment of creditors was only to be expected. They hoped they would receive charity and justice from the British Government. He said that the Venezuelan Government had good intentions towards the United Kingdom and wanted to honour her debts with her as with other foreigners, for Venezuela was aware of the danger of non-payment. In January 1862, therefore, Hilarion Nadal was sent to London, as Paez's fiscal agent, to negotiate a new loan of £1,000,000.

In his letter to Lord Russell setting out the object of his mission, Nadal explained that it was of great importance for Venezuela to obtain foreign credit, and this also applied to British bondholders, as a loan would enable a settlement to be made securing their future interests. He again emphasised the importance for British creditors that Venezuela should honour her debts. He put forward a practical solution: this was that H.M.'s Chargé d'Affaires in Venezuela should be allowed to nominate the agents who would receive, in the ports of La Guaira and Puerto Cabello, the 50 per cent of the import duties proposed to be mortgaged for the benefit of the British bondholders, and to remit the same monthly to England.

It was an extremely astute move on the part of Nadal, for he was attempting to get the British Government unofficially involved 'by the back door'. The Venezuelan Government, he stated, did not wish this request to assume the character of an international convention. He pointed out that this would facilitate the arrangement with British creditors, as it would increase the moral force of such a contract through the indirect intervention of H.M.'s Government. Both British creditors and the Venezuelan Government were now doing their utmost to manoeuvre the Foreign Office into taking up a more decisive policy. As an added inducement, Nadal stressed 'the great importance of preserving for Europe the markets so rich in products which European industry so much requires'.

The Foreign Office comment is a perfect example of their non-committal, neutral attitude: 'I am inclined to accede to this request provided no formal convention is required . . . although Nadal disclaims desire for making the arrangement an international one, he uses the words "through the indirect intervention of H.M.'s Government". There may be a risk in granting the request now asked.' This last sentence holds the key to the attitude of the Foreign Office: there could be a risk involved and H.M.'s Government were not prepared to take chances. There was no doubt that Venezuela's credit would derive great support if Russell consented, but it was argued that her credit should stand on its own merits. If they defaulted, the agency of the consuls would only be pledged in a bad cause. The Foreign Office also feared that other South American republics would feel justified in requesting the same terms when asking for loans. Nadal's request must be refused. The Foreign Office sent Mr Doveton-Orme instructions to explain to President Paez that this decision conformed with the usual practice of H.M.'s Government, and was not the result of any indifference to the needs of the Venezuelan Government. They also sent Nadal a note informing him of their decision. Despite their neutral attitude, however, the Foreign Office did not lose sight of the importance of investing in Venezuela, and realised that if this was to be successful, Venezuela had to rid herself of fiscal difficulties and protect the life and property of foreigners.

Despite Nadal's failure to obtain the help of H.M.'s Government in the way which he had proposed, he was nevertheless successful in contracting a loan in London for £1,000,000. The inducement to grant this new loan was the special hypothecation of 55 per cent of the import duties in the custom houses of La Guaira and Puerto Cabello, as security not only for the interest and sinking fund of the new loan, but also for the interest of the existing foreign debt of Venezuela. In consideration of such special hypothecation, the bondholders agreed to receive bonds in lieu of the arrears of overdue interest, and to accept a lower rate of interest on their bonds during the next three years.

A provision was included in the contract for the loan that if the bondholders or their agents were not satisfied with the sufficiency of the loan to carry out the object of its creation, and of the validity of the pledge of the 55 per cent of customs, they would be at liberty to return the money to the subscribers and to cancel the whole transaction.

Accordingly, Mr Mocatta was sent to Caracas to see that the

conditions of the loan were duly complied with. The Foreign Office also allowed Mr Doveton-Orme, Her Majesty's Consul General in Venezuela, to be associated with him, as joint agent. This consent, of course, was given privately. The Venezuelan Government published the contract for the loan in the *Registro Oficial* of 19 November 1862, and approved and ratified the contract in all its parts, promising faithfully that the Republic would fulfil all its stipulations. Under the same date, the Government of Venezuela issued another decree, which was published in the *Registro Oficial* of 22 November 1862, ordaining that for the execution of the contract in question, the custom houses of La Guaira and Puerto Cabello should set apart 55 per cent of all import duties; and that the *Pagarés* or notes of hand given by the importers for such 55 per cent of duties, should be made out separately in favour of the Custom House and of the agents appointed by the bondholders. These were to be handed over to them at the end of every week, with the proportion of any duties which might be paid in cash. Once the terms of the loan had been fully complied with, to the entire satisfaction of Mocatta and Doveton-Orme, and the funds had been applied accordingly, the 55 per cent of customs duties became the clear and indisputable property of the British bondholders.

These were excellent terms as far as foreigners were concerned, but exceedingly harsh on Venezuelans. At that time, the external debt of Venezuela amounted to £4,412,000 with an annual interest of £118,000. The nominal value of the loan was £1,000,000 but the actual loan was £630,000 at 6 per cent yearly. From this sum £214,000 had to be deducted to capitalise the interests which were due on the former debts. Venezuela promised 55 per cent on the customs duties at La Guaira and Puerto Cabello at 2 per cent per annum. Moreover, she guaranteed that this sum would not be less than £164,000 at the end of 1863, and £200,000 thereafter. As agents, Baring retained £15,000 which was owed to them as well as £12,500 for commission and brokerage. Once all these costs had been met, the Government only received 2,400,000 pesos. From this sum the Venezuelan Government had to pay the debt of the bankrupt Banco de Venezuela. This consisted of some international claims and wages from past loans. The remaining sum, which ought to have been used to pay the cost of the war, was partly stolen by officials, as was also the annual income.[1]

The country plunged into even greater economic difficulties, the army dwindled for lack of pay, there was no money and no confidence in the Government. The Federals were daily more powerful, and the failure of the loan was one of the reasons which helped Guzman Blanco in his rise to power. The repercussions which the loan had on the relations between Great Britain and Venezuela were of considerable importance. The bondholders felt that they had been cheated of their money in the latter part of 1863. The Venezuelans complained bitterly of the harsh and burdensome terms. They were convinced that the Foreign Office was 'officially' involved, since they could not distinguish between the British Consul General's private and official capacity when acting as agent for Baring Brothers. It was this misunderstanding which would persist and embitter relations between the two countries. Thus though the British Government maintained a traditionally neutral attitude, the seeds had been sown for the only occasion when the British Government could justly be accused of 'undertaking *armed*

---

[1] This pilfering of public funds had always plagued Venezuela. See Belford Wilson—Esteban Herrera, Venezuelan Secretary of State for Foreign Affairs, 12 February 1851, P.R.O. F.O. 200/26: The Venezuelan national treasury had more than sufficient to meet the current expenses of the Treasury so long as money was sent to it from the Custom Houses. It was also the case in Paez's administration: public funds were expropriated by corrupt officials, and Venezuela's financial position was weakened disastrously. See George Fagan, Resident British Minister—Earl of Clarendon, 9 April 1866, No. 15, P.R.O. F.O. 80/178. This despatch refers to money obtained from Custom Houses: 'It is beyond discussion that this sum is not a third part of what is really produced by Custom House duties'. See *The Times*, 28 January 1863. Pilfering therefore was a running sore. George Fagan (Minister)—Clarendon, 9 April 1866, No. 15, P.R.O. F.O. 80/178: Tells of a report from the Minister of Finance to Congress stating officially that the public is defrauded of two-thirds of Revenue of Customs: 'Government connives at a share in plunder.'

intervention on behalf of the bondholders' and that was in Venezuela, 1902–3.[1]

[1] D. C. M. Platt, 1968a, p. 41. For summary of *Convenio* in London regarding loan 1862, see Rojas, pp. 332, 336, 348, 350; Arcaya, pp. 226–7; Eastwick,
pp. 233–8.

Chapter 4

~~~~~

Guzman Blanco's Rise to Power: the 1864 Loan

'Lord Palmerston said with much reason that every nation had the government which it deserved.' *Buenos Aires Standard*, 18 February 1887.

Meanwhile armed conflict persisted, anarchy reigned and Falcon remained in his own province. At long last Falcon decided to send Guzman to direct the military operations – yet another step along the path to power for Guzman.

Another factor leading to Guzman's rise to power was his break with his father Antonio Leocadio Guzman. His father had backed Zamora as the surest way of gaining political power for himself. But with Zamora's death, Antonio Leocadio left the West Indies where he had been living in exile and fled to Colombia. Here he allied himself to his old friend General Tomas Cipriano de Mosquero, leader of the 'neogradino federalists'. Antonio Leocadio now tried to revive what was in fact a moribund cause, that is to say union with Colombia, in order to be able to establish a Latin Federation in opposition to the mighty Anglo-Saxon one of the U.S. In reality he hoped that this would boost his power. His ambition was so great, his ideas so distorted, that he even hoped Mosquera would invade Venezuela and overthrow Paez. Personal ambition was his motivating force, which, indeed, also inspired his son Guzman. Both Falcon and Guzman understood far better than Antonio Leocadio the Venezuelan people's aspirations.

Precisely because of this Guzman was successful in seizing the highest office, whereas his father was doomed to failure.

Antonio Leocadio's Colombian episode marks the definitive break with his son, and this in turn helped the son to free himself from his father's past. Guzman saw that his idol had feet of clay and was merely a political chameleon. Guzman had always been adept at waiting and biding his time; when Falcon's vacillations had driven his father to desert him first for Zamora, and then for Mosquera, he had abstained from any action that might have alienated Falcon. But now he saw the dictatorship collapsing, he realised the hour had come, that he had to act, to show his nationalism, and unify his country. Though the war was raging, he realised that above all the people wanted peace, and that the country as a whole desired change. Innumerable petty officials, because of their vested monetary interests, kept the war going. Nevertheless the oligarchy, as represented by Pedro José Rojas, and the Federalists, led by Guzman Blanco, saw that war could never constitute the well-being of the nation. Guzman was aware that the Federal wars had cost the country 40,000 dead and a ruined economy. On this ruin Guzman climbed to power, using Falcon to breach the gap for the first few years, while he strengthened his hold on the nation. When peace finally came with the treaty of Coche (23 April 1863), the social structure of Venezuela had been radically altered. After the war, no racial prejudice remained so that Venezuela overcame her racial troubles before many more sophisticated and advanced countries. In this aspect may be found a measure of her greatness.

Venezuela had had a full blooded revolution. Guzman found a potentially wonderful country, full of beauty and fertility but completely disrupted and unsettled. The whole government machinery was almost at a standstill, both parties were exhausted and there were no funds. The people, reputed to be one of the most belligerent of America, were really sober and industrious but poverty stricken and without an economic future. The oligarchy had left behind them this disastrous economic legacy which was to retard the country's progress for many decades. But it was this situation which Guzman would turn to his advantage.

The economic crisis, the social disintegration, and collapse of all culture, now made possible the acceptance of Guzman's tyranny, which was soon to crush the nation. Because of this, he was able to overwhelm all opposition. Falcon was an idealist, who only admitted the necessity of violence in extreme cases. Edwardes, the Resident British Minister in Caracas, considered Guzman to be double-dealing, full of self-interest and chicaneries, 'who would never have done anything whatever for British interests had he not received the most positive orders to that effect from Falcon'. Guzman was both practical and opportunist. If he found social disintegration and ruin, then the most important problem to be tackled was the country's economy. Fermín Toro had always considered that the economic factor was of more importance to the nation than a political philosophy. Guzman Blanco was able to implement his ideas and profit from them handsomely, leaving a few 'fringe' benefits for the country itself.

Guzman realised that it was 'debt' that was one of the main causes of the country's ruin. He also knew that he could and would rule if he had the money, for money was the motive force of all his ambitions. Thus power for Guzman Blanco was only an offshoot of his main ambition which was to be rich and to live in Europe. In order to attain this goal he had to establish foreign credit. 'Blanco', Edwardes reported to Russell, 'spoke much of his desire to establish the best possible understanding between Britain and his country. He laid great stress upon his desire to establish credit in Britain as by so doing he saw a vast opportunity for his country. In fact, he said, "I should infinitely prefer having credit in England to seeing one of these mountains converted into gold".' At the beginning of his 'reign' Guzman was careful not to alienate Great Britain, although he pointed out to Edwardes that Britain must be patient, for his country had only just emerged from a revolution, and that desirous as he was of getting matters straight and satisfying all just claims he did have many difficulties to contend with.

Like all Latin American governments Venezuela tended to give preferential treatment to national interests over international obligations, and there was always the excuse of the physical impossibility of meeting international obligations unless backed by the threat of force on the part of the Great Powers. The fact that the Foreign Office did not back Doveton-Orme in what was regarded as a matter of private not public interest could not have escaped Guzman's notice. Thus, Guzman's behaviour was motivated by two almost diametrically opposing forces. First of all, in order to establish credit he did all he could to obtain the sympathy and trust of foreign capitalists, relying on the fact that they wished to develop the rich resources of Venezuela. However, once he obtained what he wished. i.e. the 1864 loan, the basis of his immense fortune, he cunningly manipulated the nascent nationalism of the young republic in order to throw overboard his international obligations and strengthen his grip on the people.

There were several factors which facilitated Guzman's search for credit on the English market. 'The spirit of gambling among the English people had very much increased' and the British bondholder was both stupid and miserly. Besides, the city had good reason to disbelieve Venezuela's contention that her income was insufficient. The source of the trouble was in the country's system. One of the Government's cardinal difficulties was that the states which formed the republic were an *imperium in imperio*. They paid little attention to the Central Government and organised their rents according to their necessities. Officially the states recognised that the income derived from the Custom Houses belonged to the nation. Unfortunately enormous sums were lost because of smuggling and the compensations that had to be met. It was difficult for the British at home to believe that Venezuela's income was so affected by smuggling, but it was an indisputable fact. Eastwick also considered that Venezuela's potential mining and agricultural wealth was immense. His summing up of the situation is important since it stated the British point of view. He believed that after taking into account the resources of Venezuela, the richness of her soil, her mines, her products, and the reduced rate of her debt in comparison to what her national income should have been, Venezuela should have been well able to honour her debts. No wonder Guzman Blanco could convince the British bondholders that a further loan was good business.

As President and Vice-President, Falcon and Guzman Blanco honoured the payments on Paez's loan for two years. The 55 per cent of duties were regularly set apart and paid over to Boulton, Baring's agent in Caracas. However, in the latter part of 1863 the Government of Venezuela took $75,000 of the bondholders' funds under colour of a loan. Guzman had also expressed regret regarding the $75,000 and declared all necessary precautions had been taken to prevent a repetition. The funds would be replaced as soon as possible. This incident, however, was to affect profoundly British relations with Venezuela. The feeling of trust which had subsisted, albeit tenuously, was broken. In the words of the bondholders themselves: 'We had felt assured that the Government of Your Excellency would inaugurate a new era of justice and prosperity'. They had believed that the terms of the loan would be met punctually, and they viewed the failure with the deepest concern.

The immediate result of the appropriation of the bondholders' funds was the souring of relations between the British and Venezuelans, with the Foreign Office maintaining its neutral attitude, and the Venezuelan Foreign Ministry disbelieving it and protesting vehemently that they could not accept any intervention on the part of H.M.'s legation.

But the issue was not quite so simple. It was clouded by the fact that British officials in Venezuela were inclined to exceed their official instructions, with the understandable result that the Venezuelan Government believed they had the official backing of the British Government, even though they were afterwards forced to deny this. The confusion was increased as far as the Venezuelans were concerned when the Resident British Minister, under strict instructions from the Foreign Office, pointed out to the Venezuelan Government that their past actions 'could be most injurious to the national credit of Venezuela'. And it is on this misunderstanding between the two countries that the disastrous relations between Great Britain and Venezuela grew. Add to this Guzman's double dealings, and it is easy to realise how difficult it was for the Foreign Office to keep control of the situation and resist the bondholders' demands for official action by means of force.

With the end of the Federal wars, it was essential for the country to try and obtain a financial respite to tide them over, and with this in mind Falcon sent Guzman Blanco to London in order to try and raise a loan of £2,000,000. For Guzman this was a heaven-sent opportunity and he made the best use of it. In October 1863 Guzman signed a contract with the General Credit & Finance Company of London Ltd,[1] with the object of negotiating a loan of £1,500,000 for Venezuela. The contract was ratified by the Constituent Assembly of Venezuela in January 1864. It was a 6 per cent loan for £1,500,000 issued at 6 per cent by the General Credit & Finance Company, secured upon the total export duties.[2] The object of the loan was to 'effect a settlement of the general financial condition of the country', the building of roads, improved communications, etc.[3] It was the first time that this was mentioned as one of the objects of the loan. It was also stated that some existing claims

---

[1] Doveton-Orme—Russell, 21 January 1864, No. 3, P.R.O. F.O. 80/177: The National Convention had approved by a majority the project of a loan for £1½ million, provisionally signed in London by Guzman Blanco and General Credit Company. They further empowered the government to extend loan if necessary to 3 million.

[2] *Council of Foreign Bondholders, 16th Annual Report of Council of Corporation of Foreign Bondholders, 1939.* The securities hypothecated were the whole export duties of the Republic. In 1863, they had produced £221,500.

[3] *The Times,* 4 April 1864.

would be paid off. It was accepted by the bondholders that political strife had long been the bane of Venezuela, and it was hoped that the loan would help to counteract this. Like other South American republics, there was a tendency towards improvement; Venezuela herself was experiencing some impulse from the cotton movement. These hopes undoubtedly helped in obtaining credit.

If Guzman had acted honestly and kept his word, both sides might have profited from the loans. Great Britain could have invested sufficient capital to have afforded her a worth-while interest, and Venezuela's economic growth would have benefited the country's advancement. But because of the lack of honesty on Guzman's part, an atmosphere of distrust and dislike developed on the British side. As this became every day more and more apparent, Guzman was able to manipulate the nascent nationalism of the young republic and turn it to his advantage. It was a short-term victory, if it may be called this; in the long run it contributed to the Anglo-German blockade.

In order to gain popularity in the country, Guzman exacerbated the anti-foreign sentiments always present in a young country very conscious of its nascent nationalism. It was a particularly short-sighted policy, but one which was to have far-reaching effects as regards Anglo-Venezuelan relations. It was this attitude which caused the British bondholders to continually urge the Foreign Office to use force to protect their interests. The feeling of outrage and indignation on the part of Venezuelans would grow as they felt pressure being exerted on them. It was the breeding ground for the events which were to culminate in the Anglo-German blockade. Meanwhile the autocracy which Guzman Blanco was now about to impose on Venezuela would lead to the emergence and domination of the Andinos from 1898 to 1935.

Chapter 5

~~~

The Reasons for Guzman's Autocracy and his Absolute Rule

'It is said that Guzman Blanco intends to transform Venezuela into an Empire, with himself as Emperor.' *Foreign Times*, 5 June 1880.

'The Venezuelan experiences should be a caution to snakes and I hope will result in the Biter being Bitten.' Letter in *Evening Standard*, 20 October 1865.

On 27 March 1873 the following notice was published in the *Cosmopolitan*: 'There appeared a chief, Guzman Blanco, a man coming from the llanos, with no particular earlier advantages, but shrewd, courageous, and determined to make his way. He rose in the midst of revolution . . .' These few lines are an excellent introduction to Guzman Blanco, and his autocratic rule which was to dominate Venezuelan politics from 1870–88. Why his autocracy was possible, may be broken down into indirect and direct reasons. The direct reasons were the conditions prevailing in the country; the indirect one was the character of the Venezuelans themselves since paradoxically fighters of freedom, they nevertheless accepted Guzman's absolutism.

In his book *Tradition and Revolt in Latin America*, R. A. Humphreys describes a condition prevailing in all the continent but which is equally applicable to Venezuela herself: 'In the last quarter of the nineteenth century' he writes, 'as in the first, a great transformation, this time an economic transformation took place in Latin America. Its connections with the outside world were revolutionised. Foreign capital flowed in, to build the docks and the railways, to operate the banks and the insurance companies, and to modernise the plantations and the mines. Latin American foodstuffs and raw materials flowed out, in even greater quantities, to supply the expanding populations and industries of Europe and North America. And with the migration of capital and technology there came also a migration of people.' Though this may be said to have principally affected the pioneer hinterlands of South America, Argentina and Brazil, nevertheless the winds of change were also affecting Venezuela and rousing her people from their former ways.

Not only was this unfortunate country torn apart by civil war, but the two contending parties were exhausted, the whole government machinery was at a standstill and if Guzman was successful in his bid for a new loan from London, there would be a violent scramble amongst the innumerable military claimants who considered that as they had placed Falcon at the head of the State, they could just as easily depose him and set up one who would give them higher pecuniary inducement. Politics and commerce were nearly at a standstill. The country was struggling against financial difficulties of no ordinary character which was only to be expected after a civil war. If this continued, the country would be barred from all the benefits which foreigners and their trade were bringing to the continent. The awareness of this influenced the more thoughtful Venezuelan, but it also affected Guzman's attitude and policy towards foreigners. Paradoxically, this in turn eventually made his rule more acceptable.

It is a curious anomaly that Latin Americans for whom freedom is something lived for, fought for and died for in vast numbers, should also accept tyranny. But in the Venezuela of the pre-Guzman era the above conditions served as a kind of amalgam as regards their ideas. The Latin American heroes are *libertadores*, not Founders or Fathers. A people can never escape totally from their traditions, and in the Latin America of the nineteenth century, the traditional ruling class had objected strongly to limitations of any kind. The Latin American relied largely on intuition rather than on solid ground work as regards politics, and intellectual matters. Therefore, an upper class unaccustomed to discipline presented an infertile ground for sowing reform. Preoccupation with their prolonged struggle for political independence was a measure of the Venezuelans' sincere devotion to freedom, but it was also the cause of a certain limitation in their ideas as to the nature of freedom. Because of this, to be a *libertador* was more important than being a 'founder' preoccupied with a freedom founded on sacred laws. For the Latin American the real end of the Hispano-American independence movement, and subsequently all revolutions, was the emancipation of men's minds. Unlike their Anglo-Saxon neighbours they were not really concerned with social reforms or even economic justice. Their basic inquietude was political to be paid for with imprisonment, blood and even as a last resort death. Their background therefore precluded social reform and economic justice for the masses, and at the same time the continuation of this was the breeding ground of discontent and further revolutions. Because of all this it was all too easy for Guzman, as a so-called Liberal, to preach the necessity of personal liberty and the equality of classes as a necessary means of achieving democracy.

The extreme poverty of the people was exploited by Guzman to win them over to his cause. Then when he achieved power, he used this background of death and poverty to impose a dictatorship. The extreme, even neurotic individualism of the Latin American, contributed not a little to his being accepted as leader (caudillo) by the Venezuelans. Caudillism is a curious and fascinating phenomenon in Latin America, and in the person of Guzman particularly interesting since it explains not only why he was able to achieve power, but also the necessity of ruthlessly crushing all opposition.

A concomitant of individualism is the tendency to think in terms of oneself, rather than objectively. Therefore criticism of a policy was regarded as a personal affront, for which vengeance was unmercifully exacted. This individualism, to the Latin American, extended to all his family so that the family became more important than Society. Naturally it did not lead to political stability and resulted more often than not in nepotism both in politics and business. This in turn led to the vendetta complex which explains many of Guzman's actions regarding the railway concessions. This concept of individualism militated against a highly developed sense of responsibility to society and allowed Guzman's iron rule to flourish for so long. The 'personalismo' was inherited from Spain; it was a way of thinking and acting, the determination to rely on oneself. It may be aptly described as an exaggerated form of Spanish pride and sensitivity. It was a fundamental self reliance, which in Guzman Blanco was to manifest itself in myriad ways at both personal and institutional level, so that he was more important as a person than as a public official.

The basic contradictions to caudillism are the related elements of authoritarianism and absolutism inherited from Spain. These were the integral parts of her social and political structure, for both colonial and Church governments were authoritarian. Therefore every economic enterprise was carried along on authoritarian lines. This inheritance made it easy for Guzman to impose his economic ventures on his people, and accounts in part for his dictatorship and absolute government. Under Spanish rule, every office was a reward performed for the crown, or purchased from officers of the crown. In either event, office was looked on as a personal gift. It was rarely considered as a responsibility assumed in order to render service to the community, so that corruption became commonplace. For Guzman it was the most natural thing in the world that his public office should be seen as a source of legitimate income, and not as tainted money illegally obtained from the misuse of public trust. Such a conception, inherited from Spain, breeds a tendency to disregard legal codes when specific provisions circumscribe too closely.

This heritage is closely related to 'personalismo' or 'caudillismo' which likewise embraces patronage. The man of action, the Spanish conquistador, considered the men accompanying him to be his partners in an enterprise. On obtaining victory, the conquistador was expected to divide his booty. This explains Guzman Blanco's attitude to all the public offices, sinecures, and monopolies which he regarded as his booty to be distributed to those who had supported him during the Federal wars. This unfortunate heritage from Spain militated against a democratic form of government, and made Anglo-Venezuelan relations even more difficult as both parties found it extremely hard to understand each other.

Imported thoughts and techniques from Spain meant that Guzman could impose censorship in many ways without too much difficulty. Under colonial rule, foreign doctrines were read surreptitiously. More often than not the creole accepted these imported ideas slavishly without considering his own very important background in the cultural, educational and political field. Therefore not only was the tradition of censorship inherited, but there was often an imperfect understanding, incorrect application and in some cases confusions of political systems based on doctrines suited to other needs. Each class selected the portion he wished or gave it the interpretation best suited to his own requirements. To the upper-class creole equality meant equality before the law, but within the social class. But to the mestizo, equality meant social and economic equality for all. Likewise, liberty and sovereignty meant different things to different groups, depending on their experience and social position. General concepts were accepted but in borrowing these concepts, Latin Americans were in reality superimposing foreign ideas upon their own civilisation without due regard to the effects that these ideas would have upon their cultural pattern. As for Guzman, he used these two aspects to win over to the Federal cause all classes, and then clamped his iron rule on the country. It was not too difficult for him, for various political groups fell into even greater confusion when they tried to adopt foreign techniques of government. There was a tendency to equate national progress with a specific form of government, leading to a wide acceptance of techniques as developed in the U.S.A. Guzman 'sold' them federalism, although Venezuela's experience and tradition cried out for a centralistic form of government. Though Venezuela was a republic, her heritage demanded a permanent chief executive; *ipso facto* this meant a caudillo, a role which Guzman was able to fulfil. As Venezuela's caudillo, Guzman Blanco personified the charismatic figure in direct contrast to Anglo-Saxon institutionalism. He ruled autocratically because Venezuelans were politically immature. After years of civil war and anarchy Guzman gave the country the stability it needed through his dictatorship. These then were the direct and indirect reasons prevailing, and which paradoxically made possible the acceptance of Guzman's absolute rule.

Death had served Guzman well on more than one occasion, and it was to come to his aid again bringing him another step nearer to power. On 25 November Fagan wrote to Lord Stanley reporting the death of Monagas on the nineteenth of that month.[1] Fagan believed that there was no other person so well qualified as Monagas to secure the tranquillity of the country, and that with his death many candidates would now have recourse to arms and thus revive the horrors of civil war once again. This was to make the people turn to Guzman and then accept his autocratic rule in the hope that it would save them from even greater disasters.

With the death of José Tadeo Monagas, all attempts at reconciliation were at an end, and a policy of fierce reprisals followed. Like the able politician he was, Guzman took advantage of the situation. When he had been Falcon's Vice-

[1] Fagan—Stanley, 25 November 1868, No. 42, P.R.O. F.O. 80/190.

President he had gone out of his way to keep on friendly terms with the Monagas family. Relying on this he had returned to Venezuela in September 1868. Fagan misjudged him at the time and believed that Guzman would no longer have any influence in Venezuelan politics. However he achieved success in both the domestic and foreign fields because he came to personify all the virtues and vices of Venezuelan caudillism—a remarkable feat.

Antonio Guzman's iron rule lasted from 1870–88. These years were divided into three epochs, which were called the Septenio, the Quinquenio and la Aclamación. The Septenio is perhaps the most important and interesting since it was during these years that Guzman governed. It was when he stood out as the supreme *cacique*. The other two periods were an extension of the first, and during the latter years he enjoyed the fruits of his labours. The best illustration of how Guzman effectively terminated the caudillos' opposition is the manner in which he dealt with the rebellion of Matias Salazar, and how he finally condemned him to death in 1872. Salazar was a brilliant caudillo; he had risen from the lower ranks, and had become so predominant in the Federal wars that when they ended, he remained one of the three leading figures. At first he backed Guzman Blanco, but then he was ensnared by the intrigues of a so-called friend. Just as Pedro José Rojas had used Paez in order to achieve power for himself, Salazar now succumbed to the arguments which Felipe Larrazabal put forward. Since Larrazabal had not been given the ministry he had hoped for by Guzman, he now urged Salazar to seize power. After several abortive risings Salazar led his final unsuccessful rebellion in 1872. He was captured in May and ruthlessly executed. Guzman was determined to make an example of him because of the impact this would make on his fellow caudillos, one-time friends of Salazar and companions in arms. Guzman wanted no illusions as to what their fate would be if they opposed him. By disposing of Salazar, Guzman put an effective stop to one of the greatest dangers which threatened him, namely further attempts by the caudillos to overthrow him.

It was Guzman's aim to ruthlessly crush any force opposing him; therefore another of his first tasks was to end the power of the army. This, as he informed his ministers in Caracas, he achieved successfully at the battle of Apure. On 21 January he announced that there was no longer an enemy to fight and that he would undertake the quickest and surest way of pacifying the country that his resources allowed. It was also in 1872 that he finished the work which he had begun with the Apure campaign regarding the power of the army. He altered the institutional character of the armed forces, and dismissed the existing army and replaced it with units of 3,000 under chiefs appointed by him and also directly responsible to himself. Guzman now completely controlled all the armed forces which might have opposed him. There was a general cheapening of rank, but Guzman balanced this by a sharply increased pay scale. There was an abundance of commissioned officers, innumerable colonels and generals, but in comparison only a small trained force with practically no military education. Though the militia remained as a force Guzman did not think that it was sufficiently effective to curb the power of the caudillos should they raise their heads again, because of the practical difficulties it encountered in obtaining and organising war material. In 1879 Guzman Blanco divided the country into five districts. They were to have as their head military or national delegates whose task it was to assemble and equip military units should there be a revolt.

Before turning to Guzman's domestic and foreign policies, both of which illustrate how completely he dominated all aspects of these fields, it is interesting to note that his own character was to a large extent responsible for his success. Years before Guzman Blanco, Diego Bautista Urbaneja had informed Monagas that the constitution could be made to serve any purpose. More skilfully than any of his predecessors Guzman was to prove this point. His undoubted political genius, combined with his military talent and his understanding of how

Venezuela would react to a given military situation, enabled him to rule his country and his people ruthlessly. His personal bravery, his audaciousness as well as his theatrical manner, contributed to the magic of his success. Better than all his opponents he could impose his will and crush all opposition because of the realisation of his own strength. It was a complete revelation to him that he was superior to the other caudillos in this, and it was this self-knowledge which made him overrule his companions in arms. The Venezuelan caudillo was instinctively brave, but Guzman achieved it by will power. This made it possible for him to rule the caudillos and the army, and also subjugate them. But he failed to remove those causes which made caudillism inevitable in Venezuela. When his iron will was removed, caudillism and militarism raised its ugly head in Venezuela, and the rule of the Andinos was one of the results. This must be counted as one of his failures.

That Guzman had achieved peace within the country was a fact, but that he had done this without recourse to force and the taking away of liberty was blatantly untrue. Before Guzman, the republic only existed in name, but when he had achieved peace he could turn his attention to the administration and finances of the country. Guzman was an excellent administrator, and in his *Memoria de Hacienda* 1877, the Minister in Charge of Finances presented his accounts to the country. Guzman proposed that the country's finances should cover a period of six years, i.e. from 1870–6, and that this period should be compared to the years 1864–70. In this way a true estimate of the country's progress could be made.

Poverty had always been the country's great weakness and it was a source of constant irritation to the administration that a legitimate income should be lost because of maritime contraband trade. Not only was revenue lost, but foreign relations were soured, Guzman was quick to realise that by attacking these foreign powers, ostensibly defending the national sovereignty of Venezuela, he could gain popularity and distract the people's attention from more pressing matters at home.

In order to obtain complete subordination to his authority, he waged a fierce war on clandestine trade and contraband. He regularised and reformed customs and dues and centralised the means of collection. There was a tremendous increase in income as a result. He also dealt with the Foreign Debt as he considered this important if he was to strengthen his rule. Taken as a whole, one of the chief reasons for his success was the fact that Guzman was a first-rate administrator and organiser.

In order to put Guzman's policy towards the Church in perspective his personal ideas of grandeur must be taken into account. He concealed these under the cloak of the defence of the national honour and the rights of a weak and nascent nation which was just beginning to develop its concepts of sovereignty. He was willing to work in harmony with the Church, but only so long as their actions coincided with his. Otherwise he was determined to suppress the Church ruthlessly: he could not accept criticism.

Besides the fact that he deliberately utilised the country's ideas on sovereignty for his own ends, his relations with the Church were also affected by his belief that a nation's institutions should be secular. He admired Great Britain because she was a *secular* nation and because of the secular character of her institutions which alone enabled her to maintain a constitutional line of policy.[1] Guzman, for his part, tried to maintain a secular policy in his relations with the Church not only because of his secular ideas, but because it was against his nature to brook any opposition, and the Church for Guzman was a powerful force which could, and in fact did, oppose him. He could not tolerate a rival power within the republic, so that *ipso facto* he had to crush the Church. Historical reasons made his task easier. One of the most unfortunate colonial traditions, as it militated against stability, was the intimate union of Church and State. It meant the involvement of religion in politics. The habit of confusing treason with heresy facilitated Guzman's task, justified his actions, and confused the real issue.

[1] Middleton—Derby, 9 April 1877. P.R.O. F.O. 199/81.

One of the most interesting aspects of Guzman's autocratic rule was his foreign policy, as it had a direct influence on domestic conditions. The reasons which motivated this policy are important if one is to understand it. Also the repercussions resulting from it are far reaching. As late as 1865 a former Venezuelan Foreign Minister, Ochoa, was complaining that home politics absorbed all the activity of Venezuelans. It was a real danger for Guzman, and from the very beginning of his rule he emphasised again and again that Venezuelans must stand up to the foreigner, and not allow themselves to be crushed. Guzman deliberately incited his fellow countrymen to hate and suspect the foreigner because it was a way of channelling any opposition away from himself so that any humiliations which his government might suffer would be blamed on the foreigner, an ever popular scapegoat. At the same time Guzman was intentionally awakening the concept of nationality in the minds of his fellow countrymen. Whether he went about it in the right way is certainly open to question, but he did a great deal to bring about the growth and unfolding of his country's nationality. Ochoa had told his fellow countrymen that right is the might of the weak and if this was true Venezuelans urgently needed to define certain points in their foreign policy, e.g. the indemnities enjoyed by foreigners, territorial boundaries, treaties of amity with Great Britain, in commerce and navigation. This also applied to the other great European powers, and to the U.S. 'In the 1840s and 1850s, then, there arose a new self-consciousness in the United States, where unplanned expansion gave way in 1846–9 to the deliberate acceptance of *Manifest Destiny*. This was signified in the revitalisation of the words written for President Monroe that accompanied it. Concern was shown about the settlement of boundaries . . .'. Guzman's autocratic rule came in the decades following this, and for Venezuela it was the beginning of an era. Before this she may have had aspirations of attempting to impose her conceptions on sovereignty, but it was Guzman who gave these vague ideas form. It was a difficult task for there could be no principles of reciprocity in commerce and navigation for example, between Venezuela and Great Britain or the U.S. Venezuela was just not Britain's equal; British ships sailed the seven seas, and its flag was admitted into Venezuelan ports on the same footing as Venezuelan ships. There could be no reciprocal advantages to Venezuela if she possessed no navy.

Venezuela was beginning to be aware, as indeed Guzman was already acutely aware, that the continent of America was a vast market for foreign manufacturers. This could be a counter-balance of the use of force by the great powers against the weak Latin American nations which in the past Europe had always used against them, resulting in their temporal servitude. In order to counteract this the rights and duties of foreigners had to be re-defined. Guzman knew that it was a grave and transcendental problem, for it was extremely difficult to defend the rights of the Republic against foreign aggression. Guzman was in advance of his countrymen in that he used financial inducements, e.g. concessions, etc., in order to force his ideas of sovereignty on foreign governments. He was also prepared to take advantage of international events to further this goal. He pointed out to his Government that the war between France and Prussia was nearing its end, and that this for Venezuela meant that the markets of Europe would be reopened.

In order to strengthen his autocratic rule on the country Guzman also skilfully applied the rule of law on foreigners as well as on his countrymen. It had a twofold result: it enhanced his popularity domestically and it was a further way of reiterating Venezuela's claim to national sovereignty. The Foreign Office itself admitted that he was acting within the law. 'It cannot be denied that the Venezuelan Minister has applied to British subjects born in Venezuela, the law which Britain applies to Venezuelan subjects born in Britain.' In this field at least Venezuela was trying to secure the principle of reciprocity. It was also an established principle of the Foreign Office not to interfere, if possible, in the internal matters of a foreign country, so that Guzman was on fairly safe ground, for 'Her Majesty's

Government are also of the opinion that the general principles upon which General Blanco founds his *particular position are sound'*. In fact the Foreign Office much preferred the course of law as regards the protection of British nationals abroad. 'It does not appear why the Memorialists, if their claim is a sound one, could not take legal proceedings in the republic for the recovery of their demand, and unless such proceedings are not open to them, there might appear to be no ground for the interference of Her Majesty's Government with that of Venezuela . . . as regards legal proceedings the parties should be left to act under the counsel of their own legal adviser, and not under that of Her Majesty's Government.'

The Federal wars had been responsible for a great number of outrages on British subjects, and as a result many British claims had arisen. But Guzman was on fairly safe ground when he argued that many of these claims were exaggerated and that there were many abuses. Indeed the British Legation admitted as much. Moreover there were malpractices of British subjects in conjunction with Venezuelans. This was usually merely to make money but sometimes involved interference in the internal politics of the country if this was to their advantage. As regards the former, the British Legation strongly condemned British subjects: 'Foreigners, availing themselves of the disturbed state of the country, carried traffic into districts where it was prohibited for military purposes. These if uninterrupted carried on a thriving trade, but if meddled with, claimed the protection of their governments against losses and damages. Venezuelan subjects who did the same did so at their own risk and peril.' Because of such abuses by many foreigners, it was easy for Guzman to claim that all foreigners were trying to humiliate Venezuela, but that *he* was upholding the country's honour. It just was another way of gaining popularity, of distracting public opinion, such as it was, from domestic difficulties and last but not least of establishing Venezuela's claim to a national sovereignty. Cipriano Castro was to attempt this later, but with far less success.

Venezuela's relations with Trinidad were always particularly sensitive, and these affected Guzman's policy towards Great Britain and strengthened his autocratic rule. Trinidad herself was well aware that her trade could be altered by the internal events in Venezuela. She tried to maintain a strictly neutral policy, but it was not always easy since the Government of the day in Venezuela could well become the exiled enemy of tomorrow claiming political asylum in Trinidad. Thus she did her best to maintain the foreign enlistment act. Venezuela for her part was always plagued with suspicion that revolutionary leaders were about to launch a revolution from Trinidad, with the result that Venezuela would close the port of Ciudad Bolivar and forbid trade with Trinidad, with disastrous results for Trinidad's commerce. Trinidad also had a flourishing trade in clandestine exports of gunpowder and other materials of warfare. Venezuela naturally asked for the prohibition of export of arms. From the Venezuelan point of view the feeling of fear drove the Government of the day to attack Trinidad not only verbally but legislatively, though Guzman would have been the last to admit this publicly. In private he was fully aware that he had to restrain himself regarding the great powers: 'I do not dare claim or protest'.

Nevertheless, Guzman did help Venezuela in its struggle to assert its sovereignty. In a newspaper article in *La Opinion Nacional*, it was pointed out that before Guzman the state of the sovereign relations of the republic inspired nothing but pity and shame. But Guzman the 'regenerator' of the country with law book in hand, had shown Venezuela how to spurn foreign pretensions. He initiated a period of revindication and assertion of national sovereignty even if in the process he strengthened his autocratic rule. Guzman showed the way to Cipriano Castro in his defiance of the great powers, though Guzman had infinitely more finesse. His autocracy marked a further step in the events which were to lead to the Anglo-German blockade.

Chapter 6

❧❧

Some Aspects of Venezuelan Nationalism Regarding Foreigners' Claims and Debts
and its Effect on Foreign Relations

'I will not say to my surprise, for nothing can astonish me that General Guzman does or says.' Bunch, Resident British Minister, Salisbury, 29 December 1879, P.R.O. F.O. 80/264.

The growth of Venezuelan nationalism was to have far-reaching effects from both the short- and long-term points of view. It was important not only in domestic politics but also because of the inevitable repercussions with the great foreign powers.[1] According to the Oxford Dictionary nationalism is a 'patriotic feeling'. It generally implies a policy of national independence. Therefore the sovereignty of the country means the possession of supreme power. Like the majority of young countries, as in Africa today, the vocal and physical assertion of nationalism is the outcome of a feeling of insecurity, almost of fear, and more often than not is the result of an inferiority complex. In pre-Guzman-Blanco Venezuela, home politics absorbed all the activity of the Venezuelans. In the words of their former

[1] John J. Johnson, pp. 67 and 76.

70

Foreign Minister Ochoa, they 'lamentably neglected all that referred to international existence, as if it had not also its direct influence upon the preservation of peace and legal order, in the development of wealth and above all in the consolidation of nationality'. These words implied the awakening of nationalism, a frustrated pride in the young republic and the desire to rouse similar emotions in the rest of the country.

In 1877, according to an article in *La Opinion Nacional*, it was stated that the sovereign relations of the republic before Guzman Blanco inspired naught but pity and shame. But with law book in hand he had enabled Venezuela to spurn foreign pretensions and keep at bay the menaces of powers strong in arms but weak in right. Guzman was said to have initiated a period of revindication of Venezuela's national honour. It was also a time when Venezuela attempted to throw off the temporal servitude which she felt degraded her. On the other hand it should be remembered that when Guzman returned to power in 1879 it meant personal government of the most tyranical description, and the shameless treatment of foreign representatives. Neither of these policies would bring peaceful benefits to the country. It was circumstances that forced Guzman to vaunt his power against foreigners in order to detract from his own dictatorial methods at home, and win cheap popularity with his people, who were only too aware of their miseries and were but too ready to lay the blame on the first available person. In 1877, even before he left the presidency for a short time, Guzman took every opportunity to rouse his countrymen's anger against foreigners: 'I found a country humiliated before foreign powers, almost without the liberty of discussing its prerogatives and rights as a civilised and worthy nation, and leave it where it will arrive if my foreign policy is persevered in—to resist all injustice whether it comes from the insignificant or great and powerful'. This of course was what Guzman thought regarding his foreign policy and he was never a very modest man. Whether the long-term results were to Venezuela's advantage is certainly open to question.

As the people's economic plight was pitiful, it was fairly easy for Guzman to turn their hatred and fury from him against the foreigner, invariably pilloried as the author of all their ills. Instead of trying to give them the economic justice which was their due, he would use the official mouthpiece of the Government *La Opinion Nacional* to proclaim that he would not give a single cent for satiating the voracious covetousness of thieves— and would not cede to the iniquity with which it was sought to plunder her. In this way the exploitation of nationalism became one of the mainsprings of his foreign policy. A specific opportunity presented itself to Guzman regarding the Treaty of Commerce which existed between Venezuela and Great Britain. Bunch analysed Guzman's object as twofold: he showed his ill will towards Great Britain by being rude and offensive, and second, he attempted to expunge the Most Favoured Nation Clause from the treaty, a move which would be very popular and follow the trend of granting commercial advantages to France and Spain.[1] But, Bunch pointed out, the treaty suited Great Britain very well and they would not get another so favourable so long as Guzman exercised autocratic power in Venezuela.

Guzman also showed his ability in attacking foreigners and inciting people to patriotic sentiments of nationalism by exploiting the idea held by some Venezuelans that they were being hard done by as regards their trade, and that they were being taken advantage of by aliens. As for Guzman, he never abandoned the idea that he could obtain commercial advantages in return for political and other services.[2] It was not even too difficult to persuade the intellectual classes that if Venezuela wished to develop as a sovereign nation, she must obtain more control over her commerce.

It was this policy of 'standing up to the foreigner' that gave Guzman that magic, that charisma, in the eyes of his fellow countrymen. He sensed their desire to rule the destinies of

[1] As reported in Bunch's despatch No. 49 of 14 May 1879.
[2] Bunch–Salisbury, Caracas, 21 July 1879, No. 9 P.R.O. F.O. 80/260.

their young and inexperienced country. Even Bunch, whose personal antipathy towards Guzman was always apparent, nevertheless acknowledged that he was the right man for Venezuela.

But over and above that political sense, which enabled him to give expression to his countrymen's feelings, Guzman's psychological make-up was responsible for many of his policies. He was inordinately vain, and paradoxically suffered from an inferiority complex. He distrusted people, particularly those who surrounded him, so he crushed any opposition brutally. For years the will of this remarkable man was the sole governing force of the nation, and the hand of steel was not always covered with the velvet glove. Thus these two over-riding passions, fear and vanity, intermingled. In the words of the *Buenos Aires Standard* he was the illustrious dictator of Venezuela who became the blessing or curse of that country. Bunch, the Resident British Minister, was convinced that most of Great Britain's troubles with Venezuela were due to Guzman whom he called arrogant, supremely vain, and bitterly opposed to foreign intervention. 'It is to him that we owe all of our troubles with Venezuela', he wrote and he believed that Guzman would adopt any measure however violent, if he thought that it could be executed with safety. He also considered him to be a coward and that if bullied would fear reprisals. In the same despatch, therefore, Bunch advocated the presence of an impressive naval force at La Guaira, which could act immediately, by blockade or otherwise. This policy of urging the use of force in order to compel the young and weak Venezuela to change her foreign policy was put forward many times previous to the Anglo-Venezuelan blockade of 1902–3. It should be noted that it was not a policy which emanated from the Foreign Office, but from those diplomatic officials who were compelled to deal personally with Guzman and those who followed him.

On the other hand Mansfield, Resident Minister after Bunch, was sympathetic towards Venezuela and held that a more conciliatory tone towards Guzman should be adopted in order to relieve tension and dispel Guzman's fears. Mansfield was certain that fear was the motivation regarding Venezuela's policy towards Trinidad. Fear was always at the back of Guzman's mind where Trinidad was concerned as indeed with most of Venezuela, for from Trinidad came invasions, revolution, and bloodshed. Guzman was quite frank regarding his intentions towards Trinidad. He intended to put a stop to any revolutionary activity coming from the island, and since he obtained little visible redress from the Colonial authorities, he 'became more and more persuaded that Venezuela must find the remedy for herself'. The Foreign Office itself realised that this was the case and admitted as much to the Colonial Office, whose attitude regarding Venezuela was obviously much harsher than that of the Foreign Office. On 12 October 1882 the Foreign Office informed the Colonial Office that it appeared unreasonable to treat the Venezuelan Government, the lawfully constituted Government of the country, on the same footing as the rebels who 'admittedly use the island of Trinidad as a centre of their unlawful operations'. There could be no doubt that a few desperate adventurers had sought refuge in Trinidad and now organised raids from there on Venezuela. On more than one occasion it was pointed out to Great Britain that one of the most important and mutual duties of a state was that of not allowing hostilities within their territories against friendly nations. By allowing this to happen Venezuela was being treated as an inferior state and this exacerbated the feeling of nationalism.

But the Foreign Office answer to Venezuela's violent protests was rather different from her notes to the Colonial Office. The Foreign Office was conciliatory in the extreme, for H.M.'s Government was anxious to do all in its power to prevent any disturbance in the good relations existing between Great Britain and Venezuela. It was admitted that Trinidad's geographical position regarding Venezuela made her an obvious target for Venezuelan revolutionists planning an invasion against Venezuela, as well as other nefarious deeds, but the charge of inaction against the Government of Trinidad was vigorously denied. Notwithstanding the fact that Venezuela might have just cause for irritation against the proceedings of certain Venezuelan malcontents residing in Trinidad, the Foreign Office firmly asserted that 'there is no reasonable ground of complaint against the Government of that island'.

Privately, however, the Foreign Office pointed out to the Colonial Office that they considered the government of Venezuela under Guzman Blanco to be firmly established and recognised. It was no longer a conflict between two rival factions struggling for power, but attempts were made by revolutionaries to overthrow the Government. These revolutionaries were but a few desperate adventurers who had sought refuge in Trinidad, making it the centre of their unlawful operations as the Venezuelan Government had stated. It was therefore desirable to help the Venezuelan Government in its efforts to crush these rebels by preventing them from using the island.

Keeping in mind all these considerations, the actions of the Venezuelan Government against that of Trinidad can be justified for it must be judged against this background of fear. Even someone like Bunch, well known for his dislike of Guzman, was aware that Trinidad's actions could result in dire consequences for her. 'Of course,' he wrote to the Foreign Office 'there is not the least doubt that Trinidad and Curacao are used by refugees and speculators in the way that General Guzman describes. He himself has so used them, and would so use them again. But two wrongs do not make a right, and I venture to suggest to your Lordship whether it might not be possible to find some efficacious means of discouraging the refugees and their abettors. If we do not we shall have complications on our hands from which the island of Trinidad will suffer, as her trade with Venezuela is valuable and expensive.' Guzman therefore acted in the way which would most hurt Trinidad. Under the Conventional Decree of 4 June 1881 a

30 per cent duty was imposed on British goods coming into Venezuela via Trinidad and other West Indian Islands.

The differential duties inflicted tremendous damage on the economy of Trinidad. Apart from the economic side, they gravely affected Anglo-Venezuelan relations. Its abrogation was urged incessantly on the Foreign Office. 'It is desired that you should use your influence with the Foreign Office to get them to compel the President of Venezuela to respect treaty rights and abrogate the treaty by which he has put 30 per cent duty additional to ordinary duties.' It was impossible for British merchants to understand that Venezuela had acted in self defence believing her internal peace to be threatened by revolutionaries making use of Trinidad as their base. Thus on both sides there was a remarkable change for the worse regarding relations. 'Up to a year or so ago goods to an enormous value passed in transit through Trinidad for Venezuelan ports, and the best relations existed between the merchants of both countries. But Guzman Blanco, the President, as a simple act of malicious spite against Trinidad for affording refuge to the many whom his tyranny and oppression had driven from Venezuela, suddenly passed a decree enforcing the payment in addition to ordinary duties of 30 per cent upon all goods coming from or through Trinidad. The result of this measure has necessarily been almost stagnation in the large commerce hitherto carried on.'

Not only was there this financial aspect but also the delicate matter regarding Britain's treaty rights. The imposition of this 30 per cent duty on British goods which went to Venezuela via Trinidad and other West Indian Islands was considered by the British Government to be an infringement of treaty rights. It was repealed by decree for goods coming from Europe. But two differences now arose between the Venezuelans and the British which were to become running sores with dire consequences for Venezuela since they actively helped to embitter relations with the United Kingdom's diplomatic representatives in Caracas.

The core of the dispute between the two countries was the fact that Great Britain considered the duties to be an infraction of her treaty rights. This meant an enormous material loss to Trinidad, while the general condition of British colonial commerce with the colony was rendered precarious through continuous accusations of smuggling, accompanied by loss of revenue, annoyances and obstacles of a most serious nature to British traders. The situation was considered grave enough for Mansfield to advise Lord Granville that this matter should be settled with the least possible delay.

However, this was extremely difficult as the two countries were arguing their point of view from totally different premises. Venezuela considered that the additional duty fell equally on the goods of all nations including Venezuela herself, if those goods were imported into Venezuela from the West Indies. Consequently no different treatment existed and there was certainly no infraction of the Most Favoured Nation Treaty caused by the Venezuelan law in question. The Law Officers of the Crown argued for the United Kingdom that Article IV of this treaty stipulated 'that no higher or other duties shall be imposed on the importation into the territories of Colombia (now Venezuela) of any articles the growth, produce or manufacture of H.B.M. Dominions than are or shall be payable on the like articles being the growth, produce or manufacture of any other foreign country.'

It was therefore considered by the Law Officers of the Crown that the view put forward by the Venezuelan Government was contrary to the express terms of Article IV. If such an argument were admitted to be valid it would destroy the provisions contained in that article. They also refused to accept the Venezuelan view that Article III of the Treaty was intended to exclude the British colonies from the benefits of Article IV. Her Majesty's Government was at a loss to understand how anyone could contend, as Venezuela did, that this referred only to the flag under which the goods were imported and not to the country of their growth, produce or manufacture. In view of this, the British Government appeared to be left with only one alternative and that consisted in addressing a note to the Venezuelan Government demanding the repeal of the law, and a return of the duties levied in violation of the treaty.

Nevertheless, despite this, by 1884 there was one significant change in Great Britain's attitude. In a despatch to Mansfield the Venezuelan Foreign Minister Vicente Amengual commented with pleasure on the note received from Mansfield regarding the draft of an agreement which could be the basis of a new treaty between Great Britain and Venezuela. Its importance was the fact that 'the President of the Republic sees with satisfaction that the Government of Her Majesty is following in the course of that good understanding and cordiality which is preparing a happy solution for these and other points of difference between the two countries.' In other words Great Britain was not only going to protest, she was going to discuss, with a view to settlement, a problem which had arisen between her and the young republic. For Venezuela it meant that she had asserted one aspect of her sovereignty. It was a further step in the development of her nationality. At the same time this awareness of herself as a free and independent nation was now exploited by Guzman in his own ruthless manner regarding foreign debts. This in turn would also result in disastrous consequences for Venezuela for these debts would be one of the main, direct causes for the Anglo-German blockade. In other words it would make Cipriano Castro believe that as Guzman had got away with it, and since Britain had not used force, he too could wriggle out of his debts and difficulties by asserting Venezuela's sovereign rights.[1]

It can be said of Guzman that his personal vanity, corruption and arrogance were responsible for twisting the ideals of nationalism which his countrymen were beginning to feel. One of the most interesting and impartial commentaries on Guzman and Venezuela is a naval report by Commander

[1] See F.O. 80/259 No. 95, 10 December 1879.

Boardman. Regarding Guzman he wrote: 'He entered the capital on 27 February. His arrival was most warmly greeted by his countrymen, a large majority of whom seem to consider his presence a guarantee for security.' The following illustrates extremely well how adept Guzman was in assessing the people's political feelings. 'In the meantime he showed his confidence in the strength given him in the recollection of his former presidency by dismissing nearly all the troops, opening the ports, and sending General Cedeño (who had led the revolt) back to his post. As another instance of this I may mention that there is now no garrison at La Guaira . . . General Guzman Blanco at once commenced to repair the roads from Caracas to La Guaira . . . restored telegraphic communications, and generally set the machinery of organised government once more in motion. Business revived and merchants wrote to execute the orders which they had suspended during the revolution.' Guzman was also clever enough at this stage not to pursue political prosecutions or shoot and imprison anyone, thus winning the people over to his side as far as he could. But in his own able manner he took the significant step of publishing in the *Gazette* a nominal list of his enemies 'who had voted for the destruction of his statues'. He also published another list of his friends who had voted against that decree. The result was that those mentioned in the first list found it convenient to leave the country. The diplomatic Corps believed that Guzman's chances of achieving stability were excellent. Most important of all Guzman won over the mercantile community, for stability was for them essential. For Guzman stability was necessary if he was going to assert his country's sovereignty in the face of foreign aggressions and demands. Therefore, under his rule Commander Boardman hoped that the country would be able to enjoy 'that tranquillity which alone is needed to enable it to advance rapidly in the paths of civilisation, progress and riches'. Thus he made his countrymen have faith in him, not only because he could give them peace, but because he embodied in his own personality those qualities which they would have liked to have manifested in their own actions.

This was particularly the case regarding their attitude towards foreign powers and foreign investors. It was not easy for the mass of the people to distinguish between impartial, responsible governments abroad and often irresponsible and dishonest foreign investors and lenders, who when the nation defaulted, as it invariably did on its loans, turned its back on the republic at a time when it most desperately needed foreign assistance and skills. Thus instead of help, Venezuela was burdened with the reputation of being financially unsound and dishonest. By behaving as they did, the foreign investors indirectly contributed to the economic anarchy which was unquestionably a factor in Guzman's power as a caudillo. By 'standing up to the foreigner' Guzman was speaking for his country. At the same time he was contributing to the awareness of Venezuela as a nation by asserting her sovereignty. This was part of his role as a charismatic leader, whose importance in Latin countries should never be underestimated.

Venezuela's debts were distinct from the recognised diplomatic claims. Both debts and diplomatic claims were the most important matters affecting Great Britain's relations with Venezuela. They were also the means by which Guzman asserted his own ideas regarding his country's foreign relations. This generally meant that he would brook no interference from outside however justified this might be: 'General Guzman said that if my doctrine were accepted the sooner the British subjects left a foreign country the better, as it would be perfectly unbearable if the British Government were to collect their debts.' Two more important points emerge from this despatch, for these were the overriding ideas which coloured Guzman's policy towards foreign nations and towards Great Britain in particular. The first was that as the debt was to private creditors it was purely a matter of internal administration. Consequently no foreign government or representative had a right to interfere. The second was that anyway Great Britain would never interfere, and as a general rule she allowed such creditors to suffer the consequences of their own imprudence. It is not surprising, therefore, that Guzman failed to honour these debts since he did not fear the consequences. This attitude in Venezuela continued to exist and greatly influenced Cipriano Castro at the turn of the century. It had become part of Venezuelan nationalism.

The recognised diplomatic claims were as follows. The first comprised those arranged in 1865 between the then Resident British Minister, Mr Edwardes, and the Venezuelan Minister for Foreign Affairs. It was estimated that they amounted to about £70,000 including interest in May 1879. The second set of claims were those established to the satisfaction of a mixed commission in 1868–9. In May 1878 these were estimated at about £50,000 including interest. A certain proportion of the Venezuelan Custom receipts, thirteen unities of 40 per cent, was nominally set apart for payment of the recognised foreign diplomatic claims, and were to be divided periodically *pro rata* to the rest of the creditor nations.

As regards the first class of claims, those of 1865, the British Government felt that they had a special grievance. The Venezuelan Government had tried in every possible way to evade its liability for them. The Foreign Office therefore found itself in the predicament of paying nothing to those claimants for whom they had received no money from Venezuela, or of paying them out of the sum calculated on the amount of the 1868–9 claims, which would have been hard for those latter claimants. Consequently nothing was paid.

With respect to the second class of claimants, those of 1868–9, the complaint was that the periodical payments were frequently suspended, and portions were kept back on various pretexts. They ceased with the revolution of 1878, but with Guzman firmly established once more in 1879, the Foreign Office believed that the payments would be resumed. The matter however was further complicated by the Venezuelan Government pleading 'our necessities of conservation and progress'. It was proposed that there should be an issue of bonds in payment of diplomatic claims, such bonds to be secured on 13 per cent of 40 unities. Bunch's remark regarding this proposal was that Guzman himself had told him that if the British and other creditor nations did not meet his wishes, he would simply distribute the 13 per cent of the 40 unities amongst the creditors in proportion to their claims and do no more. It was a case of the debtor imposing his conditions and the creditor was not even to be heard. This however was not the Venezuelan point of view, as Rojas explained to Salisbury. Rojas stated that his Government's plan consisted in the issue of a diplomatic debt for the said approximate amount at interest of 3 per cent per annum to be delivered by means of the legations to the respective creditors. This would be under the guarantee of a solemn compact with the creditor governments or their representatives at Caracas. They would hold at their absolute disposal the produce of the 13 units. The legations would undertake to receive it from the National Treasury to apply it periodically to the payment of the coupons and to the redemption of the capitals.

It was emphasised by Rojas that his Government wished to arrange the affair in the manner most satisfactory to the creditors. He thought that the proposed form was unquestionably the most appropriate because it offered to foreign governments payment in a permanent manner until the complete extinction of the claims. It was hoped the British Government would accept this. By June 1880 it became obvious to the Venezuelan Government that Bunch was not only not supporting their proposal, but was actively reporting against it. Venezuela did not wish to create unfriendly relations, but this had happened because she had defaulted as regards her claims and debts. 'My Government', Rojas explained at considerable length, 'which ardently desires the firm friendship of that of Her Britannic Majesty, and seeks with eagerness how to meet its exigencies has instructed me to offer to your excellency every necessary explanation to do away with the erroneous view which unfortunately disunites the two Governments in this affair'. He pointed out that it was not Venezuela's intention to withdraw from the fulfilment of her obligations. He emphasised that regarding the claims of 1865 and 1868 arising from the civil wars, the period for their payment had never been stipulated, neither had Venezuela ever consented to grant them the benefit of interest. Therefore it could not be said that Venezuela had failed because she was paying more slowly than expected.

Venezuela did not possess the resources for living as well as paying her creditors. The current estimate, which Rojas enclosed, showed the extremely small revenue available. This was proved by the scantiness of the salaries, by the poverty of the services, by the reduction of the army, and by a large number of economies. This meant that the Government had to be very careful in order to be able to provide for the administrative and fiscal necessities of the financial year with the limited produce of the public taxes. The Government's chief preoccupation was that due to Bunch's despatches, serious conflicts could arise. And he reiterated that 'there can be no conflict between two Governments which correspond with each other in good faith, and which have lived for fifty years in harmony'. All that Venezuela had done had been what Great Britain would also do under the same circumstances, i.e. pay all creditors *pro rata* without conceding privileges to any one, and in order not to harm them by the delay, grant them the benefit of a yearly interest.

Venezuela was also faced with the difficulty that Great Britain was not the only creditor nation. At that particular time France was agitating violently claiming preference because the convention she concluded with Venezuela in 1864 was prior to that concluded with other governments. Rojas pointed out with some truth that if Venezuela were to accede to the demand of the French Government there would be no possibility of paying the British Government a single cent for years. Spain, the United States, and Germany, Holland and Denmark had all concluded conventions with Venezuela, and claimed their money. Venezuela's main object was to pay the interest for her debts, in order to enjoy the credit which she required for the development of her prosperity and to grant that interest to her creditors in compensation for the delay in payment of the principal. It was hoped that Great Britain would realise that this was the only way that Venezuela could faithfully carry this out, in conformity with the law, and above all without involving herself in international complications.

The bedevilment of having to meet a number of creditor nations affected Great Britain as well as Venezuela. The principal difficulty in this matter, commented the Foreign Office, arose from the fact that so many other countries were interested, and independent action on the part of Great Britain might give offence to them, while joint action was difficult to arrange. Bunch, the Resident British Minister in Caracas, could not view the matter as dispassionately as the Foreign Office. And from his despatch it is obvious that his intense personal dislike of Guzman Blanco blinded him to the many genuine difficulties which Venezuela faced. As far as Bunch was concerned there was only one remedy available in order to obtain the money required to pay British claims and creditors and this meant the use of force, 'for we shall have to deal with the man who is the genius of Venezuelan dishonesty'.

Bunch was convinced that Venezuela would pay at three days' notice, if it were positively demanded by Her Majesty's Government, and he thought this sum could be raised with the assistance of the mercantile community as the merchants would prefer to hand over their money rather than see diplomatic relations broken off and a blockade instituted. To make sure the money was paid Bunch suggested the presence of a squadron 'as a proof that we are in earnest'.

But should peace measures fail, a blockade of the River Orinoco and of Ciudad Bolivar alone would soon procure the money in question. He was convinced that British creditors would never see a shilling of their money back, except under

84

compulsion. In a further despatch Bunch insisted on the use of force: 'I regret to say that I see but one possible way, viz., a peremptory demand, supported by a distinct intimation that force will be employed if justice should be refused.' He admitted that this action could lead to a rupture between the two countries, 'but if no punishment is ever to follow such gross breaches of faith as Venezuela habitually commits, never more so than in the present case'. This very fact that Great Britain did not take action, and did not use force even though it was so strongly recommended, had long-term results. When Cipriano Castro had to face similar demands by the British Government at the turn of the century, he did not believe that Great Britain would act, keeping in mind the events of the past. He thought that the reasons which had kept her from using compulsion would be strong enough to restrain her from such action. As regards Great Britain, Bunch's continuous advocacy of the use of force served as a reminder that this might be the only efficacious method of obtaining redress. His phrase 'if no punishment is ever to follow' foreshadows the Roosevelt corollary after the Anglo-German blockade. What is obvious with hindsight was totally ignored by Guzman and his successors up to Castro: this was that in the long run their country could not assert its nationality or even be sure of its sovereignty if its debts exposed it to the threat of force. Guzman by his bullying and blustering really clouded the issue for his own countrymen. They could only see that he got away with it. They failed to realise that he had never tried to tackle the heart of the problem, which was to pay off the country's debts and then develop Venezuela's sense of nationality free from the danger of force and compulsion. From this point of view Guzman's policy was a total failure for he only retarded Venezuela's sense of responsibility and in consequence her assertion to sovereignty.

As regards the Foreign Office they were in a predicament. They were aware that Bunch's plan regarding the use of force would settle the matter once and for all, but there were objections to this use of force against Venezuela. France, the United

States, Germany, Spain, Holland, all had claims on her. All were entitled to share in the monthly payments on account of foreign claims. If the Venezuelan Government yielded to Great Britain's demands, they would make this an excuse for their inability to pay the claims of other nations. If the British Government were to blockade the Venezuelan ports all revenues from customs would cease, and no payment could be made to foreign creditors. If on the other hand the Custom Houses were seized and the revenue collected, then the other nations would have a claim against Great Britain for the instalments due to them.

These were only a few of the problems which would follow should force be employed. One of the gravest difficulties was that they realised they were in extremely bad company regarding the many claims made on Venezuela, for a large number were fraudulent, a fact which Venezuela also knew. It is significant that Bunch, who had no love for Venezuela, admitted as much. 'There is not the slightest doubt that these claims are grossly fraudulent' he wrote. In the same despatch he reported that the Spanish Minister had admitted to him that there was not the slightest doubt that Spanish claims were 'grossly fraudulent'. He also explained the reasons why Guzman had increased the allowance to Spain to the detriment of the other creditor nations. According to the Spanish Minister *less than* 10 per cent of the claims were actually held by Spaniards. The bonds were the property of Venezuelans, notably of General Guzman himself, who had received a third (about $500,000) at the time of their issue by Rojas who had made the arrangement, and by the Government clique. The Minister of Foreign Affairs bought $48,000 of them just before the new distribution of monthly payments. For these reasons it was not likely that Spain would join in any attempt to coerce Venezuela.

Regarding the United States, this was even more delicate a problem. 'The United States', commented the Foreign Office, 'the largest claimant, would undoubtedly look with great jealousy on any attack upon Venezuela.' Her claims, like those of Spain, were also greatly exaggerated. Bunch was certain that frauds had been committed by the two commissioners aided by the United States Minister of the day in Caracas. The Government of the United States did not admit the fraud but it declined to acquiesce to a fresh commission. It was therefore improbable that she would coerce Venezuela. 'Its hands are not clean' as Bunch so graphically put it.

Holland's claims were also fraudulent since Guzman and his Foreign Secretary made an arrangement with the principal claimant, a Curacao Jew. Bunch genuinely believed that the Government of the Netherlands was not aware of the robbery which was being connived at by its subjects, as there had been no representative in Caracas since the rupture of diplomatic relations, but the truth would come out if coercion were attempted, which was unlikely. As for France, the Foreign Office merely remarked that as they were acting in concert with her as regards those claims, it was scarcely courteous to take an independent line without consulting her. But Mansfield, the new Resident British Minister who took over from Bunch, was not quite so restrained. He was horrified concerning 'the abomination of French claims'. In 1864, the French representative, when these claims were being prepared for settlement, appeared to have a large personal interest. Most of the claims for which he obtained recognition were fraudulent, and of those claims for which Mellinet (the French representative) had not received money, more than five-sixths were believed to have been of a fraudulent character. The sum claimed beyond the losses incurred was ten times the amount. The truth of this unsavoury story had been verified by Bunch, Middleton and the Resident French Minister himself.

Aghast at what was being forced upon them the Venezuelan Government saw this as an excellent opportunity to assert its sovereign rights, and therefore the present President, Guzman, was sent to Paris to negotiate. General Guzman had stated that he was almost treated with brutality by Drouyn de Lhuys who had told him 'après le Mexique ce sera votre tour'.

According to Guzman he there and then signed under protest that Venezuela could not sustain such a burden. So much for 1864. But what should never be forgotten is that these frauds were known by Venezuelans. They were fully aware that these so-called 'honest' European powers were not above 'crooked business methods' and that moreover they were prepared to defend their so-called rights with the use or threat of force. They were also aware that British claims on the whole were 'clean' and that because of this the Foreign Office did not like to align itself too openly with the other creditor nations. All these considerations were to affect Castro at the time of the Anglo-German blockade. As far as Guzman was concerned he used these circumstances, favourable to himself, to appeal to his fellow countrymen as an honest patriot defending his country's rights against the usurping foreigner.

The attitude taken by the Foreign Office was that of wait and see what policy Guzman himself would adopt towards his foreign creditors. By 15 April 1881, the position had deteriorated sufficiently for France to present an ultimatum to the Venezuelan Government respecting the settlement of the diplomatic claims. The Chargé d'Affaires fixed the period of eight days for the acceptance of French conditions. As Venezuela rejected this ultimatum, the Resident French Minister, the Marquis de Tallenay, asked for his passports and placed the French citizens resident in Venezuela under the protection of the Italian Legation.

In the opinion of Mansfield it was impracticable for the Venezuelan Government to yield to the French ultimatum, especially as the term of eight days was fixed as their limit. Besides which it soon became obvious that the Executive could not have acted otherwise since public opinion and the country supported Guzman in his policy of not yielding to French threats. 'Even the President's enemies thoroughly support him in this crisis and no doubt rests upon my mind that any other decision would have been productive of serious discontent if not of overt revolution.' So much then for the sense of nationalism which was awakening in the country and which Guzman was using for his own personal benefit. The people for their part felt they were resisting an injustice, and that the internal sovereignty was being threatened.

The Foreign Office were now placed in a very difficult position. The objection against the use of force, advocated by Bunch, was mainly that it was not practicable even though it might have been justified. Above all, complications with the other creditor nations became more apparent every day. The United States was their main preoccupation: 'especially the U.S. always jealous of foreign action across the Atlantic'. A mere suspension of diplomatic relations, unless followed by coercive measures, would be futile. It could almost be counter-productive. Mansfield himself was of the opinion that Bunch's attitude, as well as that of France, had only resulted in arousing fear in the mind of Venezuelans, with the consequent result that they felt that their internal sovereignty was being threatened. He believed a more conciliatory attitude would produce better results. The Foreign Office were convinced that if the French were allowed to take hostile action without Great Britain, she would make exorbitant demands and leave no money for anybody else. They were not the only ones to fear the consequences of the use of force. The foreign creditors of Venezuela, represented by E. P. Bouverie, explained the situation and the resulting pitfalls. With the breaking off of diplomatic relations with the French, the Venezuelan Government feared that they would impose a blockade so as to put pressure on them. If this took place, British trade would be stopped and the payment of the debt would be interrupted. These consequences would inflict severe injury on British interests. Bouverie therefore trusted that the Foreign Office would do its best to prevent such an occurrence. There was little doubt that behind the scenes Guzman was doing everything he could to outwit the French. 'Do not forget to inform the British creditors', Guzman had written to O'Leary, 'that should France blockade us or take any other measures of the sort, Venezuela will be unable to comply with the last settlement of her external debt, which is being carried out with exemplary exactitude. Amongst the creditors there are persons of importance, and it is impossible that they cannot have sufficient influence to induce the British Government to interpose their good offices to save their interests from an act of notorious injustice.' When it suited him Guzman was willing to forego Venezuela's sovereignty. Once more the Foreign Office officially adopted a strictly neutral attitude. They felt it was undesirable that neither the British nor the French Governments would be represented in Caracas and thus the rupture of diplomatic relations was ruled out. But in their instructions to the Resident British Minister in Caracas, the Foreign Office maintained its past position and refuted any suggestions from Mansfield himself that perhaps the Venezuelans were right and that they had never agreed to the claims which were being exacted so ruthlessly.

Mansfield himself, the new Resident British Minister, believed Great Britain had everything to gain and nothing to lose if she bided her time and awaited the results of France's actions against Venezuela. If Venezuela should give way to French pressure, British claims, resting on solid and honest foundations, could participate in any advantage and Britain might even obtain better terms. On the other hand should Venezuela hold out, it would then be evident that coercion was ineffectual, and that Guzman could count on the support of Congress as well as that of the country. Guzman believed concessions could lead to revolution and internal disasters. Mansfield himself realised that Venezuela faced a number of difficulties. The Government was disconcerted at France's action. Guzman assured Mansfield that he would like to give preference to British claims which had been regulated with such astringent rectitude, but that unfortunately he was bound to France technically, even though French claims had been a tissue of fraud and dishonesty. Guzman pointed out that action taken regarding one set of claims must apply equally to all the others. This was only one of Venezuela's innumerable difficulties. The Federal revenue, exclusively derived from customs duties, if attacked by the French, would lose everything. The French ultimatum itself had already resulted in a deterioration in the value of property, in government paper money and the rise of prices. Several mercantile houses were already countermanding all European orders executed. The low price of coffee also contributed to the extreme poverty. Despite all this, Venezuelans, both friends and enemies of Guzman, stood behind him. There is no doubt that their sense of nationality had been awakened not by any love of Guzman, but by the use of force against them. Meanwhile as far as the United Kingdom was concerned, with the sympathetic Mansfield as Resident Minister, Anglo-Venezuelan relations did not fare as badly as Franco-Venezuelan relations.

It was to Mansfield's credit as a diplomat that he did everything in his power to help towards an amicable solution of the affair with France. The Venezuelans themselves were aware of his conciliatory attitude, and he was asked to help by Guzman's father himself, A. L. Guzman, now 'a very old man indeed', and invariably employed by the President in all really confidential communications with foreign Legations. But even at this early date it was not British but American power which was of more importance to Guzman. On 26 April 1881 Mansfield informed the Foreign Office that the President had telegraphed to the Venezuelan Minister in Washington to solicit the Government of the United States to 'prevent hostile action upon the part of the French Republic'. Guzman also telegraphed a second time to the United States Government asking them to neutralise the action of the French Government towards Venezuela. The United States replied that the instructions which Guzman desired had been transmitted to the United States Minister in Paris. The request for American help was dangerous, a double edged sword as far as Venezuela was concerned. Guzman was blatantly asking the Americans to interfere when his country got itself into financial difficulties with the great European powers. From the despatch it also appears as if

Mansfield realised only too well the wonderful opportunity which had been given to the United States to assert her sphere of influence. 'It will be interesting to know', he wrote, 'whether such friendly offices may not be a screen to cover a significant intimation that European interference in this continent, even when the case be fairly legitimate, is far otherwise than agreeable to the Government of the United States.'

By July of the same year the United States had gone one step further; she was now hopeful of being able to superinduce a settlement, honourable alike to both nations. The United States Government was disposed to undertake the office of trustee at the suggestion of Venezuela. She would receive and distribute the monthly quota among the creditor legations, subject to the consent of the powers concerned, and upon the indication that the Government of Venezuela would devote a larger sum towards the liquidation of their engagements; the latter, however, being dependent upon the acceptance of the first condition. The United States Government declared that it did not incur any guarantee or liability, but merely offered their most friendly offices, and not as a restraining influence on France.

The main difficulty arose when the French Government declined the proferred trusteeship of the United States, on the grounds that their claims upon Venezuela possessed a priority over those of other creditor nations. While the U.S. was asserting her power and sphere of influence, at the behest of an American republic, France, unlike Great Britain, would not accept her good services and did not fear offending her. Mansfield was left with the hapless role of trying to persuade the Venezuelan Government of the futility of fastening their hopes upon the dream of foreign mediation. He saw that he had to convince Guzman that the core of the problem lay in settling the debt and not postponing its payment. Otherwise the road would be open to the use of force. By 1882 the situation had become stalemate. The French Government hoped that the Venezuelans would take the first step, which Guzman would certainly never do, as it would spoil his image in Venezuela as regards his foreign policy. Guzman hoped that when Monsieur Gambetta came to power he would help in making the French abate their terms and come to a satisfactory arrangement, as he considered him to be a friend of his. But nothing was done and the open sore continued to fester. The French Government were even said to have told Venezuela: 'une fois et pour tout de bon était décidé d'en finir avec les ennuis Venezueliens'. Guzman well knew that after such a long lapse of time since the withdrawal of their representative, and with so much else upon their hands, the French were unlikely to resort to coercive measures towards Venezuela. As was usual with his foreign policy he managed to win the short-term round but must be held seriously responsible for the disastrous foreign relations once he was gone. By not paying, and by deliberately invoking United States influence, he manoeuvred Venezuelans into a sort of euphoria that they could continue to 'get away with it' as long as they were backed by American power.

In his dealing with the great European powers Guzman not only acted in an arbitrary, rude manner, but he also tried to obtain the support of other American republics for his so-called intercontinental policies. He convened a semi-official conference of the South American states. His object was based on Bolivar's own idea of a close union between the Spanish American communities. Guzman suggested the adhesion of the United States for a mutual guarantee of their respective territories on the principle of *uti possidetis* in 1810, and it was hoped that they would agree to refer all their differences to 'arbitration' and regulate other subjects of international interest.

Every aspect of the nation's life was twisted and turned to suit his own ends, and this was generally done under the guise of upholding Venezuela's sovereign rights and deliberately inciting her sense of nationalism. Very often it was quite a trivial matter which was blown up out of all proportion as in the case of the assault on the Italian Minister, which resulted in diplomatic relations being suspended between the two countries.

From the financial point of view, Guzman managed to manipulate every aspect of national life in order to assert Venezuela's sovereignty against the foreigner. For example he issued a decree by which $800 were to be deducted daily, until Congress met some time in February, from funds belonging to the external debt. The object of the deduction was to furnish Congress with a bank of territorial credit so as to develop agriculture and the breeding of cattle. In other words Venezuelan agriculture would be under deep obligation to Guzman's Government, even though this had been done at the expense of her foreign debt. But Guzman was a past master in manoeuvring his so-called Venezuelan debt settlement in order to pocket more money himself under the popular cloak of asserting Venezuela's sovereign right. Guzman also took care to lay much stress upon the development of public works. One of his chief objects was to sell concessions, but of course always with the excuse that this would enable Venezuela to develop her resources and assert her sovereign rights. By making his country his chief victim he was directly responsible for the worsening of her foreign relations, and sowing the seeds of future discord with the great powers. The *Financial News* warned its readers that it had its eye on the General's 'concession factory ever since it opened for incidents such as these could only result in the most unhappy consequences for Venezuela; it would not be surprising if the French authorities would feel called on to intervene for the protection of French citizens whose credulity had been too successfully practised by the "Illustrious".'

But Guzman took care to emphasise that the relations of the Republic with foreign powers was satisfactory because in this way he won the people's confidence, yet in the same breath he stated that he had set in motion the question of the disputed boundaries between Venezuela and Colombia and British Guiana and Venezuela. Though he stressed the fact that he had bestowed on Venezuela the greatest of all benefits, pride in herself as a nation asserting her sovereign rights against all foreigners, he nevertheless left his country burdened with a disastrous legacy in so far as her foreign relations were concerned. As Mansfield put it: 'Venezuela is the home of paradox' and as long as Venezuela remained the sport of this remarkable man his schemes of self-aggrandisement could only result in future trouble for his country.

Last but not least his policy of appealing to the United States for help when he thought his country threatened by European powers was pregnant with danger for all the Americas. 'The United States has had many occasions of applying the doctrine *Civis Americanus sum*.'

Chapter 7

The Reaction: Failures of Democracy and the Repercussions on Anglo-Venezuelan Relations

'A plague on both your houses for whichever side eventually comes out "on top" as they say in America, British interests must suffer.' *Capitalist*, 13 August 1892

'There are a large number of persons who feel perfectly well qualified to fill the exalted office of President. But the President's chair can accommodate only one at a time; enlightened "personalismus" convinced many practitioners that even in politics moderation is a virtue.'[1] President Linares Alcantara[2] represents the attempt of propelling Venezuela away from the outmoded wars of the nineteenth century towards progress, however slight, and the oncoming twentieth century. He also represents Venezuela's failure, and its far-reaching results at home and in Anglo-Venezuelan relations.

There was no doubt in the minds of many foreigners and Venezuelans that Guzman Blanco's autocratic rule had brought many benefits to his country. In 1874 *The Bullionist* wrote that

[1] *The Times*, 11 October 1892.

[2] Francisco Linares Alcantara, 1877–9. Linares Alcantara was to have been Guzman's puppet president installed in office to keep the presidential seat warm for him while he, Guzman, enjoyed Europe. Unfortunately for Guzman, Linares Alcantara was a man of independent mind with ideas of his own.

under the presidency of Don Guzman Blanco the country appeared to be making progress and that profitable concessions for the advancement of the country had been granted. In 1877 *The Bullionist* was to write once more regarding the progress that had been made under the able rule of Guzman Blanco. He had imposed peace where before revolutions were of frequent occurrence. It was also remarked that the change of presidency from Guzman Blanco to Linares Alcantara had been effected constitutionally and without bloodshed, 'a fact that was rare in the annals of the Republic'.

Despite this seemingly rosy picture, however, the reality was somewhat different. On 1 June 1877 the *Star and Herald* reported that considerable excitement, and what at one time threatened serious trouble, was occasioned in Caracas during the last days of Guzman Blanco. The sessions of Congress were unusually exciting and several debates were characterised by exhibitions of great intensity of feeling between the adherents of the great political parties. Attempts were made to intimidate the adherents of Alcantara. The Government of Guzman Blanco resigned power very unwillingly, although the elections should have been sufficient proof of their unpopularity. Guzman Blanco himself acknowledged that his Government was a dictatorship. The election of Linares Alcantara was a protest against that form of government and evidence of the universal wish of the people for constitutional rule.

The fact that the new President was considered 'one of the liberals of Antonio' did little to dispel the fears that the elections were not conducted fairly, and that Guzman Blanco would continue, under the name of another man, as the governing genius of the Republic. Despite this, the very change of government encouraged the reaction that was to take place against Guzman Blanco and reach its peak in 1889. As the *Star and Herald* remarked: 'all liberal-minded people would be delighted that the reign of Guzman Blanco had ended and that the military despotism of a quarter of a century that had oppressed that unhappy country had been abolished.'

The state in which the country found itself when Linares Alcantara took over was to have many repercussions. The new Government considered it its duty towards the nation itself as well as towards friendly nations, to issue a statement regarding the position in which it found itself upon assuming power on 22 March 1877.

At that date the Treasury was found to be in considerable debt to the amount of 1,092,097.18 *Venezolanos* of which an amount of 350,293.04 *Venezolanos* had been paid off on 30 June 1877. The principal liabilities consisted in those occasioned by advances from the Bank of Caracas, public works, immigration. Enormous sums had been spent on 'the furniture of the most sumptuous character' for the Presidential Residence, and arrears of interest upon bonds. It was emphasised that an attempt had been made to pay the debts of the Republic with regard to foreign nations.

The fact that Venezuela's relations with foreign countries were far from satisfactory was to constitute a further factor in the failure of democracy, since these only increased the Government's difficulties in its attempts to govern. Among these the suspension of relations with Colombia regarding territorial limits influenced the politics of the State of Los Andes and the resulting unrest weakened the Central Government's power. The disagreement with the U.S. proceeding from Venezuela's protests against the awards of the mixed commission of 1867–8 augmented the Government's difficulties *vis-à-vis* their foreign policy. As seen in the previous chapter the most serious troubles with foreign countries were the result of non-payment of debts, and this had short- as well as long-term results. Thus all these economic and political difficulties curtailed the new Government's freedom of action.

Much the same picture applied to Venezuela's relations with Great Britain. Various complaints had been put forward by Great Britain because of the obstacles placed in the way of the departure of English ships destined for Curacao. The closure of the ports of La Vela and Maracaibo and its effect on British shipping exacerbated feelings between the two countries. It was also remarked that the Treasury possessed no surplus accruing to foreign claimants because it had been appropriated to other purposes by the last administration. Attempts were also made to reduce the number of men under arms as well as curtailing public expenditure.

It has been said of Linares Alcantara that his chief contribution was that he sponsored the reaction against Guzman Blanco's autocracy. His failures, however, outweigh his success in that his reforms were only superficial. He did not tackle the heart of the problem so that the country was continually exposed to the dangers of dictatorial or weak rule. Perhaps one should not judge him too harshly for he was at least conscious of his country's wish for some measure of liberty, and its desire to cast off the thraldom imposed by General Guzman Blanco and the terror which it had disseminated. Linares Alcantara also made some attempt to adopt a less dishonest line of policy in regard to financial matters, than that which had been practised during Guzman's seven years of autocratic rule.

Nevertheless the fact that Linares Alcantara merely tackled the outward signs of the problems with which he was faced was obvious to the British Legation as early as 18 September 1877. As yet the British Legation could see no reasonable motive for the belief that the new President was making a genuine attempt at democracy, for the measures he undertook were in reality nothing more than concessions to potential and/or genuine agitators and adventurers whose support Linares Alcantara could not afford to forfeit. The Resident British Minister did not think it was due to public opinion since no such thing could exist in the Venezuela of that time.

The measures restricting public expenditure in the field of concessions were but palliatives or sops to greedy and clamorous agitators who were active in their abuse of Guzman Blanco. Their hatred was satisfied in so far as Guzman's pecuniary interests must have suffered a little. For example there was the withdrawal of the concession of the railway line from Caracas to La Guaira. Nevertheless Guzman Blanco was still extremely rich. It was commonly reported that he held about £2,000,000 in English securities, in addition to a large rent from land property. He received a pension of about £3,000 per annum for life from the State.

Since the core of Venezuela's economic difficulties arose from her foreign debts this automatically worsened Venezuela's foreign relations with the creditor countries.

Furthermore as the British Minister believed that these debts could have been met easily by some payments, tension and distrust were the inevitable result. Another proof of Linares Alcantara's failure in tackling the country's economy was his policy towards trade. Again corruption and contraband trade was the main reason for this. The House of Boulton & Co., through one of its branches established there, was at the head of the immense contraband trade carried on. Boulton was further implicated in unusually large profits regarding the coining of nickel money, of which large amounts were smuggled into Venezuela from Westbury, U.S.A.

Thus the evil genius of Guzman Blanco still presided in Venezuela despite the change of government. The robbery and corruption which should and could have been eradicated by Linares Alcantara continued to flourish, which naturally influenced his domestic and foreign policy. At home this wholesale robbery was accepted. In the words of the British Minister: 'without even the faintest murmur and exercised with perfect impunity'.

But despite the fact that Guzman's evil genius continued to flourish in many ways, nevertheless his departure had definitely helped to precipitate the reactionary movements which had been simmering under the surface for so long. There is no doubt that most young countries with unfulfilled social, economic and nationalistic goals will more often than not resort to revolution. In Venezuela the keynote for the exercise of power at this stage of her history was 'caudillismo', but at the same time the lines of the State were rational and idealistic. Therefore for

Linares Alcantara, nicknamed 'the great democrat', there was the added compulsion of trying to legalise his position through the constitution. In this way he attempted to take advantage of the reactionary elements, and sought to maintain his power seeking constitutional status.

There were two electoral aspects which must be considered at that time. The technique of 'continuismo' was attempted by Linares Alcantara. That is to say he tried presidential domination by extending his term of office. Guzman Blanco on the other hand achieved alternation in office. He successfully practised the 'paternalistic' caudillo's policy of allowing someone else a term in the presidential seat, just because he felt sufficiently secure, and because there were a great number of people in his debt, being financially and politically beholden to him. Therefore it was in their interest to back him. This desire to extend the presidential term of office legally or by force, was to be one of the burdens Venezuela was to suffer until Romulo Betancourt. It had both domestic and foreign implications since 'revolutions were really only a more violent species of a general election. Usually the President wants to stay in office beyond his allotted term and the only way of resisting his unconstitutional desire is by use of force'.

Linares Alcantara's brief experiment, one might almost call it a flirtation with democracy, was soon over. On 30 November 1878 he died suddenly; his death altered the course of events completely, even though he had only attempted to liberalise the country superficially.

The 'interim' period which followed Linares Alcantara's death was only important in that the difficulties which had beset him loomed even larger given the added prospect of Guzman's return to power. In Bunch's opinion, Linares Alcantara's administration had been weak and ephemeral. The situation, as far as Great Britain was concerned, would now be much worse, for under the circumstances Guzman was certain to succeed as dictator. And it is to him 'that we owe almost all our troubles with Venezuela'. Guzman was arrogant, vain and bitterly opposed to foreign intervention, but he would fully understand the implications in the use of force.

If this was Bunch's belief, however, it was certainly not that of the Foreign Office. It was this difference of opinion between H.M.'s diplomatic representative and the Foreign Office regarding the use of force, which clouded the issue as far as Venezuela was concerned. Between the Resident British Minister's fiery words and H.M.'s Government actions, there was a world of difference. Therefore Guzman Blanco had never believed that force would be used in order to exact payment. With this example in mind President Cipriano Castro drove the British Government to this very impasse prior to the Anglo-German blockade. Castro never thought the British Government would resort to force. This then may be one of the long-term results of both British and Venezuelan foreign policy.

After Linares Alcantara's death there was not even the farce of democratic elections; there was but one candidate for the presidency, General Guzman Blanco. The press which existed was controlled by the Government, and was actively brainwashing the public by describing *ad nauseam* the swift progress which the country was making. Nevertheless Bunch believed that beneath this seemingly quiet surface reaction did exist: 'It is quite notorious that great uneasiness prevails' not only in Caracas but in the interior.

There were, however, some undercurrents of reaction, but these were due to deep-seated economic fears for the future. These were duly noted by Bunch since this alarm had political implications regarding Guzman's foreign policy. On 26 September 1879 Bunch informed Lord Salisbury that a French commission had arrived. It was to study the general capabilities of Venezuela from a financial, an agricultural and a mining point of view. It was understood that an arrangement had been made between Guzman and the General Transatlantic Steamship Company of France, of which Mr Pereire, the banker, was Chairman. Though there was nothing definite, it was proposed that the company should become the possessor of the various schemes and concessions which Guzman had allotted profusely to his family and friends, e.g. immigration, railroads, gold mines of Caratal, gas, tramways, a bank, and other minor enterprises.

In return for these concessions, the company was to advance or to expend sums amounting to 20 million francs. Bunch noted two things: (1) that Guzman had provided for himself handsomely in the arrangement should it come to anything, and (2) that it had caused profound dissatisfaction to the present cabinet and the mercantile body of Caracas: 'we have been sold to a French Jew'.

A further despatch from Bunch to Salisbury referred to this contract. The agreement was to be between Señor de Rojas and Pereire; the company, in conjunction with the Government, would have the sole right to establish a mint in Ciudad Bolivar, in Caracas, or any other place.

This would convert into the national coinage all the gold and silver of Venezuelan mines. Consequently the Government prohibited the exportation of all gold and silver. It was Bunch's belief that these concessions would cause great dissatisfaction in the State of Guyana for many private interests would be injured by it, notably the various mining companies, British, American and native.

The political implications of these concessions did not escape him, particularly as it affected the colony of British Guiana. He was also aware that these important arrangements had been carried out in Paris, without consultation with Caracas. This in itself was further proof, if proof were needed, of Guzman's dictatorial rule and the failure of democratic government in Venezuela. As far as the United Kingdom was concerned, Bunch judged that if Guzman's plan were successful, it would have serious implications. If the whole mining district were made over to Pereire and his associates, Venezuela would still preserve her territorial jurisdiction and nominal sovereignty, but a colony would be formed of purely French origin and directed by French interests. They would practically control the whole of the territory which bordered on British

Guiana. Consequently all foreign competition would be excluded. French influence would be paramount. Great Britain would have a powerful neighbour instead of a weak one.

The French Government would undoubtedly support French interests in the event of complications between Venezuela and any other country, 'ourselves for example'. It was Bunch's opinion that this was at the back of Guzman's mind, for he well knew that the weak spots of Venezuela were the mouths of the Orinoco and the gold mines of the State of Guyana. Though Bunch enumerated the advantages which would accrue to Great Britain if this territory were taken by force, believing that it was entirely within Britain's grasp, nevertheless he did not propose to invade the State of Guyana. He merely wished to point out the dangers which the United Kingdom would have to contend with, if this project were to be successful: Great Britain's position would be neutralised by the establishment of the virtual sovereignty of France over this valuable portion of Venezuela. Thus he pointed out that Guzman's plan was to have at his side a powerful ally should any other foreign power be disposed to assert its rights. As regards Venezuela he would have 'sold out' the most valuable and accessible of the possessions of Venezuela without as much as an 'if you please' to his fellow countrymen.

Any resentment regarding Guzman Blanco's actual return to Venezuela could be attributed partly to the unpopularity of his French project in Guyana. This popular feeling he disdainfully ignored completely. Guzman was also criticised for the failures of all his schemes in Europe. For example he had failed to settle commercial treaties, as well as all foreign and diplomatic debts.[1]

[1] Opinions seem to differ as to whether Guzman's return was popular or not. Perhaps one of the best comments may be found in a commentary of the *Sporting Times*, 3 January 1880: 'the people of Caracas are a canny and far-seeing race. They had resolved to erect a statue to the President of the Republic, but as the President changes as often as the moon, they have had the head made so that it unscrews. Thus the same body and the same horse will do for any amount of Venezuelan Presidents.' This commentary is an excellent example of the contempt with which Europe regarded the young American republics.

The public was aware that his trip had been reduced to providing for the return of his family at the public expense and this had cost Venezuela at least £20,000. But the country was powerless to stop him. Not only did Guzman completely ignore public opinion, but the ministers he chose were mere puppets: 'the individuality of any minister of General Guzman Blanco is so effaced by the force of his will that the antecedents of the official are of no consequence'. Linares Alcantara's rule had not lasted sufficiently long to establish a number of men with ideas of their own capable of opposing Guzman Blanco's will. As regards her foreign policy Venezuela would be at the mercy of any President ignorant of international affairs, but caudillo enough to impose his will in Venezuela. Once more the failure of democracy, and the pathetic effort to react against autocracy, had far-reaching results. The brief, ephemeral period of 'relaxation' was over, and from 1879-84 Guzman Blanco ruled.

It is interesting to note the significance of Guzman's accession to power as regards Venezuela, for with him all pretence, all attempts at democracy vanished. Venezuelans realised that they were back to square one, for no democratic advance had been or could be made. From now on Guzman had only one purpose, and that was to destroy any vestige of freedom that might have survived his predecessor's death. 'He had endeavoured to put down political discontent by means of random and ruthless imprisonments carried out in most cases in a very tyrannical and illegal manner. The consequence is that there are now groaning in the dungeons of Caracas and La Guaira a large number of citizens. And yet Venezuela is supposed to be a Republic with the fullest enjoyment of civic liberties and rights, and where freedom of speech and of the press is declared by the law to be the birth-right of every Venezuelan citizen.'

Without entering into too much detail at this point, it is important to note Guzman's manoeuvrings regarding Venezuela's debts. Each and every move was calculated to strengthen his grip on the country's finances, and to get the better of his foreign creditors, a move which would help his 'image' at home. What he proposed was to assimilate the internal and external debts to the point of complete identification. The debt of Venezuela was to consist of £4,000,000 of which £1,250,000 would represent the home and £2,750,000 the foreign debt. If this plan were admitted, the two debts would be identified, and the bonds of the one would be sold in the foreign markets, exactly like the bonds of others. There was no doubt that Guzman Blanco thereby calculated on foisting the external debt of Venezuela upon the London market. The plan could scarcely commend itself to the holders of the bonds of the external debt. This unification of the internal and external debt raised an entirely new question. Such an arrangement would not only be unfair to the holders of the latter inasmuch as the internal debt had no special securities. It would certainly lead to the whole of the new bonds being gradually transferred to the Venezuelan market, when excuses would be found for further compromise, if not for blank repudiation.

The Council of Foreign Bondholders themselves had no illusions regarding Guzman. They realised no reliance could be placed on his word, and subsequent events justified their prediction. Guzman's manoeuvrings on this aspect of the debt can be traced as early as 1874 when a general meeting of the bondholders rejected his proposal that it was a *sine qua non* that the execution of an agreement could only take place if the construction of the railways from Caracas to the coast had previously been secured by the raising of fresh capital for that purpose. At this point it was emphasised that the Council had continued to receive favourable attention from the Foreign Office on the few occasions when they had requested assistance or information. It was then not considered desirable to cause trouble to H.M.'s Government, or to seek intervention for trivial purposes. *And Guzman was fully aware of this.* Like the bondholders, he knew that in the long run hostile intervention harmed commerce, and created dangerous complications. The bondholders had experienced great embarrassment by the interruption of diplomatic relations in the past, e.g. with Mexico. Therefore, since the Foreign Office had so many opportunities for rendering solid service not only to the bondholders but to the national interests confided to its care, any untimely call was to be deprecated. The bondholders had previously stated that they had received great assistance from H.M.'s representatives, when they had been authorised to receive payments or supervise collection of securities. But this also was to cloud the issue as far as Venezuela was concerned. Once British officials became involved, even unofficially, it became impossible for Venezuelans to distinguish the niceties of the case. This would ultimately create greater problems.

As far as policy was concerned it was not only in his handling of the Venezuelan debt and railway concessions that Guzman excelled; gold mining in Venezuela attracted much attention and several new companies were formed. Gold mining was increased and capitalists were attracted, all to the benefit of Guzman himself. Gold mining was particularly popular at this date and Guzman took every possible advantage. As a reader of the *Money Market Review* remarked in a letter to the Editor: 'The coming craze for mining companies is evidently going to be in the direction of the gold districts in the various parts of the world . . . those which have been fully developed in Venezuelan Guyana, are now exciting very general attention, more especially in consequence of the marvellous success which has attended the working of the "Callao" gold mine in Venezuela by a private company established in London.' The *St James's Gazette* also pointed out that Mr Bunch's (Resident British Minister in Caracas) report to the Foreign Office had stated that the gold mines of the Caratal district in the state of Guyana continued to be very productive. New gold fields had lately been discovered near Pastora; they were of extraordinary richness and exceeded those which had hitherto been worked. Everywhere the hand of Guzman could be found behind a new enterprise or new development. His financial hold on the country was total for he owned or directed most enterprises which could and did yield money. This state of affairs was recognised and acknowledged by the Council of Foreign Bond-holders in their annual report of 1884. It was here admitted that when General Crespo took over the presidency on 27 April 1884 the prosperity of the country had increased and capitalists were much attracted because of Guzman's able rule.

These then were but some of the aspects of Guzman Blanco's administration from 1879–84. They serve to highlight only too well the superficiality of the reaction against his former autocratic rule. Guzman's continued dictatorship demonstrated Venezuela's failures in democracy, failures which would cost Venezuela a very high price. Eventually, and because of this failure, the Andino faction would be able to impose years of absolute, autocratic rule. The beginning of the end would come with Gomez's death in 1935, but true democracy would have little chance of survival until Romulo Betancourt gave it to the country.

It seemed to Guzman that when his term of office ended a military man might be the best person for his particular paternalistic type of caudillismo, a caudillo who delighted in 'alternation' in office, i.e. someone who would take over and keep the presidential seat warm for him.

Military service was an excellent medium for the expression of 'personalismo' in all its forms. The only problem was to find a military man both capable and loyal. Such a person was Joaquin Crespo.

Guzman could hand over the reins of power because he felt so completely secure. This enabled him to afford the luxury of allowing someone else a term of office as President. In this, his first attempt, he was successful because of Crespo's loyalty. This first period of Crespo's rule is characterised by his sub-servience, and his Government was little more than a 'caretaker' one. Guzman chose well when he left Crespo as President. His other candidates were to prove less satisfactory from his point of view. Guzman had every good reason to trust Crespo, for when Linares Alcantara had first mooted his project for extending his presidential term of office Crespo raised his voice in protest by publishing 'In defence of the April cause'. It was remarkable in that its publication demonstrated courage and independence of thought all too rare in those days. Moreover, after Linares Alcantara's death it was Crespo who distinguished himself militarily in defending Guzman Blanco, thus assisting his return to Venezuela most effectively. It was also Crespo who kept Venezuela 'loyal' to Guzman over the Pereire affair, which could have affected Guzman's cause adversely.

Meanwhile when the time came for Guzman to allow presidential elections once more, he was extremely reluctant to do so. The constitution provided that Congress should meet on 20 February and immediately proceed with the nomination of the Federal Council, by whom and from whom the President of the Republic was elected. Guzman Blanco employed the delaying tactic that the necessary quorum had not presented itself. This had happened because the obligatory number of members, who were in their places for the opening of the session, received a hint to go away for a while. Guzman himself cared little that his actions savoured of illegality. In the words of the Resident British Minister: 'treating the matter with indifference which would have been appropriate had he been discussing any unimportant arrangement of ordinary life'.

The real cause of the delay was that the opposition party, although comparatively powerless, was extremely numerous and planned a revolt if the election of the new President had taken place at the date prescribed by the constitution. But since their funds were meagre, the unexpected delay made it impossible for them to act. In Mansfield's opinion it was obvious that the Federal Council must elect as President one of Guzman Blanco's nominees. There were two: one was Señor Rojas Paul, who had been Guzman's Minister of Finance. Mansfield considered that Rojas Paul carried little weight in the country, but was honest and respectable. The other candidate was Joaquin Crespo, staunch adherent of Guzman. Crespo, however, was of moderate intelligence and ability. He possessed no experience of government and office work. Though Guzman would have preferred Rojas Paul, there were plenty of intrigues to promote Crespo's election. Though Crespo might be honest himself, it was surmised quite correctly that he would be unable to prevent others 'from taking liberties with the public purse'.

On 15 April Mansfield informed the Foreign Office that Crespo had been unanimously elected President. Despite the fact that Crespo was a follower of Guzman, nevertheless his election was considered a partial rebuff to Guzman, for he would have preferred Rojas Paul as being more compliant to himself. Meanwhile Crespo's task was to 'hold the presidency' and to carry out Guzman's views until the latter was again elected for the next presidential term.

There is no doubt that Crespo's character affected his domestic policy and consequently his foreign policy particularly with the United Kingdom. He was an adherent of Guzman and a prominent member of the 'Liberal' party. He had a reputation for honesty and if he had been left to himself he might conceivably have managed. But once Guzman was out of the way (Guzman was leaving the country for London as the Venezuelan Minister) Crespo fell under the influence of a camarilla of unscrupulous persons, already well known for their mercenary and ambitious designs. The fact that Guzman had been much feared during his long tenure of power (nearly fifteen years) meant that his many enemies would try to take their revenge; it was more unlikely that Crespo would be able to restrain them. Guzman had always exercised strict control over everyone as regards public funds, but now that this vigilance would be relaxed, the greed of hundreds would have to be satisfied. Once the iron rule of Guzman were removed, it was Mansfield's opinion, as well as that of others, that revolutionary incidents of some magnitude would take place before the end of the year. It was Crespo's weakness of character which now directed the course of events. Those who felt they could aspire to political power and possessed some independent opinions, turned to their only known source of redress for past wrongs, revolution and fighting. Only two comments can be made regarding Venezuela at that date. Such people or parties whose fate was linked to that of the new or old caudillo cared little for the peace of the nation. In the words of Eduardo Galo Plaza three-quarters of a century later, the world would soon be 'witnessing a demonstration of the national sport'.

There is no doubt that Guzman foresaw his successor's difficulties, not only at home but abroad. It was important for Venezuela, as well as for Guzman Blanco, to improve relations with the United Kingdom. This Guzman tried to do before he handed over the presidential office. On 15 March the Venezuelan Foreign Minister wrote to Mansfield that the 'Illustrious American', having the welfare of his country at heart, desired as proof of his love for the same, to present to his fellow citizens the settlement of pending questions between Great Britain and Venezuela. In this way he felt he would be able to secure a permanently friendly understanding between the two countries. According to Guzman this had been one of the principal objects of his administration. Judged impartially, there is no doubt that Guzman desired a settlement, but in conformity to his own ideas, irrespective of right or justice. Therefore the Resident British Minister was advised that one of the first acts of the next Government would be to fill the post of the Venezuelan Minister in London, and that it would be he who would conclude the negotiations.

On 30 April the press in London reported that Mr Anderson had asked the Under-Secretary of State for Foreign Affairs if the negotiations with Venezuela had as yet resulted in the abandonment of the 30 per cent differential duty imposed on British goods, in violation of the Treaty of 1825. It was rumoured in Trinidad that H.M.'s Government was considering a deal by handing over to Venezuela the small British island of Patos. Lord Fitzmaurice replied that H.M.'s Government had submitted to the Venezuelan Government certain proposals regarding the differential duties. As to Patos, if the questions at issue were satisfactorily settled, the question of Patos, which was but a rock, would be favourably considered.

On 31 May 1884 the Venezuelan Foreign Minister referred to the British proposal. The important point in this document was that the Venezuelan Government noted with satisfaction the acceptance by Great Britain of Venezuela's viewpoint, which to Venezuelans implied that their country's sovereignty was being asserted.

The document ended by informing Mansfield that it would be the Illustrious American (Guzman Blanco) who would be the Venezuelan Minister in London and conclude the negotiations. This is an excellent example of how Guzman Blanco contrived to keep the real power within his grasp. It was becoming obvious that Crespo's Government would only be a caretaker government.

But these were not the only difficulties which Crespo was to encounter very early on in this, his presidential term of office. By May 1884 the British were complaining that the Venezuelan Government had no right to say that no funds were available for the purpose of converting the internal debt, when already this large sum had been handed over to them. The *Statist* considered that it was more serious than mere incompetency, for it had the appearance of embezzlement. Already the rapaciousness of Crespo's friends at home was being felt abroad. In British eyes there was nothing to do but to accept the 3 per cent which Venezuela could clearly pay until the assigned revenues increased sufficiently to cover the promised 4 per cent. As the *Statist* remarked bitterly: 'creditors of a foreign state are powerless when governments prove indifferent or refractory'. It was the seeds of this bitterness, accumulated over the years, which would eventually lead to the Anglo-German blockade and the Roosevelt corollary.

Even nature itself seemed to be against Crespo; Venezuela was visited by a plague of locusts which caused great damage and despoiled verdant plantations. Added to this, there was the low price of sugar and a resultant depression. The very peace of the country was threatened especially in Guarico, the birth-place of Crespo. There were fears of war, of the country being invaded, and Guzman Blanco himself was rumoured to be on his way back to Venezuela so that his military skill 'may once more reduce his country to subjection'.

Crespo's weakness as ruler was confirmed in Mansfield's reports to the Foreign Office. On 19 June 1884 he reported that he considered Crespo too weak to be the caudillo, and too un-democratic to help to establish democracy. He allowed his associates to despoil the country financially, and revolution once more reared its ugly head. Chief of the revolutionists was General Pulgar, long regarded as one of the most important of rebels. Crespo believed he could placate Pulgar by sending him abroad and at the same time keeping him quiet. Pulgar availed himself of his lucrative appointment in order to leave the country safely, and go to Trinidad without exciting suspicion.

Thus Trinidad again became 'unquestionably the base of revolutionary intentions'. Mansfield was only too aware of the dangers facing Trinidad should the revolutionaries use the colony as a spring-board. Anglo-Venezuelan relations would then rapidly deteriorate. 'It is to be presumed that the authori-ties in the colony are well aware of what is going on and will be prepared to intercept any overt acts of a filibustering character.' Unfortunately Mansfield's worst fears were to be confirmed.

In England Guzman Blanco took as active a part as he was able in order to defeat the plans of the revolutionists, thus showing once more where the real power lay. Guzman called on the Foreign Office and requested that a telegram should be sent to Trinidad asking the authorities to keep strict watch on General Pulgar, and take all the measures consistent with British law to prevent any acts which could endanger the peace of Venezuela. If this could be done, there was an excel-lent chance of peace being preserved. Moreover, it was pointed out by Guzman that the commercial community in Trinidad was desirous that peace should be maintained and that the conspirators should be discouraged. Guzman fully recognised the danger which threatened his 'caretaker' Government and in his usual energetic way he attempted to repair the damage caused by Crespo's weaknesses.

Venezuela's minor caudillos, however, were not to be put off so easily and in November Mansfield warned Trinidad's Governor that a bevy of rebels was now assembled on that island. These were Generals Pulgar, Pulido Mendoza, Level de Goda and other well-known conspirators against Crespo's Government. Pulgar was considered to be the 'chief of the revolution' and the sum of $150,000 (£24,000) had been guaranteed by two wealthy Venezuelans. Arms were also said to be on their way.

Crespo's Government believed that the rebels were to obtain a steamer in Europe or St Thomas, and that piratical attacks would be made on the vessels entering and leaving the Orinoco with gold from Guyana mining districts. Therefore, apart from the piracy which was threatened, Mansfield realised that most of the mines in the district were owned by British companies, and thus British interests could be seriously affected. It was once more a question of a weak domestic policy exacerbating Anglo-Venezuelan relations. In order to try and remedy the already strained relations between the two countries, Venezuela decided to send to Trinidad Mr O'Leary, brother of the late British Vice-Consul in Bogotá. Since Mansfield could not commit the Governor of Trinidad to any immediate action Venezuela's hopes of influencing H.M.'s Government now rested with Guzman Blanco in London, further proof of his enormous power and influence in Venezuela. It was also Mansfield's considered opinion that in despatching O'Leary to Trinidad, the Venezuelan Government had acted with energy and discretion. But whatever the outcome, Trinidad once again became involved in Venezuela's revolutionary plots. This also served to highlight Crespo's weaknesses and foment the fears which all Venezuelan Governments had when the peace of the

Republic was threatened. And it was this fear that clouded Venezuela's judgement regarding its relations with the United Kingdom.

As for Crespo's domestic policy, perhaps one of the best and most charitable descriptions may be found in the following comment: 'Men fought to gain public office; they tried every possible manoeuvre to obtain their goal and every subterfuge to achieve their ambition'. Crespo could barely contain the many caudillos restless for power, but as his was only a care-taker government he survived and for his pains received the title of 'the hero of duty'. On 2 October the *South American Journal* reported that General Guzman Blanco had arrived at La Guaira on 27 August. Venezuela had for some time been preparing for the return of the Illustrious American. The whole country knew he would soon be taking up the office of President once again. According to the press Guzman's return heralded a series of ovations and rejoicings. This is an excellent commentary on the utter failure of Venezuela's first attempts at democracy. She had tried to throw off the shackles imposed by Guzman's absolutism. She had only succeeded in an interregnum, and a weak caretaker government, with a consequent worsening of Anglo-Venezuelan relations.

Chapter 8

'They Were Neither Up Nor Down'

'The grand old Duke of York,
He had ten thousand men;
He marched them up to the top of the hill,
And he marched them down again.
And when they were up they were up,
And when they were down they were down,
And when they were only half way up,
They were neither up nor down.'

This old rhyme illustrates perfectly the situation in which the various Venezuelan Governments found themselves from 1888–99.[1] It would have needed a first rate administrator, as well as a scrupulously honest man, to have hauled Venezuela out of her financial quagmire. Instead of which the country was beset by opportunists on the one hand and would-be revolutionists on the other. 'Palacio', said he, 'has one foot in the stirrup, and the other on the ground, and he is just watching to see which way the horse will jump.' As for the rest of the country, it was a common saying that 'everyone is a revolutionist except the President'. These then were the two great problems which faced Venezuela during those years, and which not only affected her domestic policy but which had far-reaching results in her relations with foreign powers.

[1] Presidents: Juan Pablo Rojas Paul (1888–90), Raimundo Andueza Palacio (1890–2), Joaquin Crespo (1892–8), Ignacio Andrade (1898–9).

116

As far as Great Britain was concerned relations (unofficially, as diplomatic ones had been broken off since February 1887)[1] tended to be cold. The Foreign Office preserved a remote and strictly correct attitude. For example, when the North American Squadron enquired whether there were any objections to their visiting the ports of La Guaira and Puerto Cabello, the Foreign Office commented that they would be inclined to say that they should abstain for the present. Nevertheless the Foreign Office was thought to be on far too friendly terms in the eyes of many British subjects, even if these were only official ones. 'I can scarcely believe' wrote an outraged victim of Guzman Blanco's, 'that the honourable traditions of British diplomacy would permit the holding of communications with a man like Guzman Blanco . . . whose utterly unscrupulous and tyrannical acts have brought ruin and desolation amongst many innocent people.' Yet throughout these many difficult years, despite many provocations, official Foreign Office behaviour remained strictly correct. It can be summed up as an attempt to settle amicably the various pending difficulties between the two countries. The fact that in the long run the Foreign Office failed to establish better relations may be to a large extent attributed to Venezuela's disastrous economic position. The norm which ruled the actions of the Foreign Office is embodied in the instructions given to Boulton, British Consul in Caracas: 'It is important for us to go into the merits of the question; our only attitude must be that of desire that the matter be amicably terminated without injustice to the British interests involved.' And this correct British behaviour continued to guide the actions of the Foreign Office throughout this period of suspended diplomatic relations.

---

[1] *South American Journal*, 5 March 1887: 'H.M.'s Government have received intelligence that diplomatic relations would be suspended between H.M.'s Government and the Republic of Venezuela on 21 February. The cause of the suspension is stated to be the difference about the frontier between British Guiana and Venezuela.' See also *Financial News*, 18 March 1887: 'diplomatic relations suspended—grave event'.

During Crespo's presidency Guzman Blanco had himself appointed to the post of Envoy Extraordinary and Minister Plenipotentiary to various courts of Europe, specially created for him, with the special object, as he, Guzman, declared, of settling all questions with the various powers to which he was accredited. These resulted in failure: 'a complete failure, very particularly with regard to this country.' Unable to gratify his vanity by having the glory of settling the pending difficulties between the two governments, Guzman returned to Caracas in 1886, having been called again to the office of President of the Republic.

Guzman felt that his dignity had been wounded and his vanity checked and he had left Great Britain full of resentment. Politically this was to have repercussions, for from then on relations between the United Kingdom and Venezuela became unusually strained over the disputed boundary in Guiana. 'Venezuela', wrote the *Daily Telegraph*, 'is not a country in which the majority of Britons take much interest, but it gains an unwonted importance just now from the fact that a serious dispute has arisen between Great Britain and an equatorial republic. That quarrel is due to conflicting claims to a region which has suddenly acquired an enhanced value from its auriferous capabilities.' The result of this state of affairs was that Guzman Blanco suddenly broke off relations with H.M.'s Government in February 1887, as already noted. The Foreign Office believed, and with reason, that Guzman had succeeded in convincing the Venezuelan Government that he, and he alone, could satisfactorily settle the difficulties which existed between Venezuela and Great Britain. Yet it was his evil influence which remained one of the chief stumbling blocks, and it was productive of the most disastrous and far-reaching consequences: '. . . it may be truly and justly affirmed that it is almost exclusively owing to his policy and bad governing counsels that the rulers of the country have been influenced in their relations to foreign powers, walked in the same road mapped out by this dictator . . . to pursue a policy so thoroughly detrimental to the true interests of the country and diametrically opposed to the principals of international equity and of justice.'

Guzman Blanco's presidential period, 1886–8, is known as the *Aclamación*. This may be said to represent the fruition of his past years in office. As far as Venezuela's relations with Great Britain were concerned, this period is dominated by the breaking off of diplomatic relations, the frontier dispute and the claims in connection with the vessels *Henrietta* and *Josephine*. These continuous disputes, however, had the long-term effect of souring relations between the two countries, and they exposed Venezuela to the dangers of the great powers imposing their will by force. The legacy which Guzman Blanco handed to his successors was to prove a heavy burden.

As early as 10 November 1887 the *Morning Post* stated the necessity of settling the disputed boundary question of British Guiana, for it was 'important to imperial and colonial interests alike' and it was not yet decided as diplomatic relations were still suspended. Moreover, Guzman's period of office was fast drawing to a close and in a few months would have run its course. The name of his successor was unknown even in Venezuela, but already many candidates were preparing for the post.

Despite all her many difficulties Venezuela was considered to have advanced with rapid strides both socially and commercially since the consolidation of the foreign debt in 1881. It is interesting to assess Venezuela at this point. The vast resources of her territory were becoming more widely known, and the financial houses of Britain and France were contributing to the development of the immense wealth concealed beneath Venezuelan soil.

The person chosen by Guzman Blanco as his successor as President of Venezuela was a civilian: Juan Pablo Rojas Paul (President 1888–90). As early as 9 April 1888 Guzman Blanco was busily writing from Paris to his followers in Venezuela that at long last he could see his party being reasonable since they had elected Rojas Paul. In Guzman's own words: 'my entire co-operation will not be found lacking. You can rely on it'. He was loth to quit power. The election had aroused difficulties and opposition. It had been rumoured for some time that the former President Joaquin Crespo also aspired to be re-elected. When he realised that a satisfactory arrangement could not be arrived at, Crespo resorted to Venezuela's customary recourse, a call to arms. Crespo had tried to put himself forward as a candidate not so completely under the influence of Guzman as Rojas Paul appeared to be. But from Paris Guzman *insisted* on the confirmation of Rojas's election to the presidential chair.

Meanwhile opposition to him was assuming the ugly appearance of a civil war. From Great Britain's point of view the fact that Crespo took up residence in Trinidad heralded a series of demands and refusals from both Venezuela and Trinidad embittering relations even more between the republic and the colony. 'The Crespists,' wrote a Trinitarian Serjeant Major, 'have taken possession of the *Bolivar* and are shooting the crew.' Meanwhile an armed party of police was out to retaliate. This, however, only served to infuriate the Venezuelan rebels as well as the Venezuelan Government which constantly complained of the inadequacy of Trinidad's measures against the revolutionists. As was usual on such occasions the Foreign Office maintained a strictly neutral policy. 'I do not want any Colonial Office action' wrote Salisbury on his commentary adding with relish: 'Do not let us stop attacks on Guzman Blanco more than we are obliged to do.' He obviously thought of Rojas Paul as being Guzman's tool.

Nevertheless, as far as Trinidad was concerned, she faced a difficult problem, for the Government of Venezuela urged the necessity of the condign punishment of the rebels and the expulsion of all Venezuelan refugees from Trinidad. In his letter to the Venezuelan Minister for Foreign Affairs, the Governor defended Trinidad's attitude, which in Venezuelan eyes was lack of co-operation. He stated that he was unable to expel Venezuelan refugees as England had always afforded asylum to political refugees, and that policy was enforced in her colonies. The fact that the twelve Venezuelans under arrest were being proceeded with under the law, plus the promise that the Government would try and prevent ¦any infringement of the foreign enlistment act was certainly not sufficient to quieten the fears of the Venezuelan Government, fears which undoubtedly inspired most of Venezuela's action against Trinidad.

From then on it was a question of whether the Venezuelan Government would be strong enough to crush the revolution and install Dr Rojas Paul in office. Rojas Paul was to prove a much stronger ruler than either Guzman or his opponents had suspected. He dealt swiftly and successfully with the rebels. He granted an amnesty to political offenders and freed the lately captured chiefs of the insurrection. This had the beneficial effect of creating throughout the country a feeling of goodwill and respect towards Rojas Paul. At the same time he won the appreciation and support of Crespo, who shortly after his release embarked for Buenos Aires.

By this magnanimous and statesmanlike gesture, Rojas Paul diminished Guzman's chances of a return to power in Venezuela. Moreover he proved his independence, showing he was not Guzman's pliant tool as everyone had suspected. Most of Venezuela's statesmen heartily disliked Guzman, but unfortunately they disliked and mistrusted each other too much to combine to keep him out, besides which they had most of them at one time or another been in his pay, although he always kept so much of his bounty for himself that they remained dissatisfied. This was a weakness with which Rojas Paul undoubtedly had to cope.

By June 1889 Guzman Blanco was also aware that Rojas Paul was no accomplice of his and he was soon busy writing from Paris to his friends in Caracas urging them to choose candidates for the convention who would not be friends or complices of Rojas Paul, whose policy had become one of extreme reaction against him. Already Guzman Blanco was planning who the next presidential candidate would be and he hoped it would not be a friend of Rojas Paul. Meanwhile Rojas Paul himself was proceeding vigorously but diplomatically against the absent Guzman. In order to sever the ties which bound him to Guzman because of his election, Rojas Paul now took the extremely astute step of resigning. If he was to continue as President, his mandate must come from the people and not the former dictator. The whole of Caracas was in an uproar and everyone tried to make him change his mind, but he issued a bulletin announcing his acquiescence to the people's wishes. Merchants and shopkeepers backed the action. Rojas Paul expressed his gratitude for the demonstration but his guarded phrases disappointed all who expected he would frankly express his intention of a complete break with Guzman against whom a most bitter feeling prevailed. Rojas Paul was too clever to place himself in jeopardy; instead he adroitly allowed his private opinion to be leaked.

Despite all doubts and misgivings Rojas Paul was to prove his worth. Soon Andral wrote to Salisbury announcing Guzman Blanco's resignation as Minister Plenipotentiary in Europe. It was believed his resignation would not be accepted. Nevertheless, the country led by Rojas Paul now took its stand against Guzman. This showed exceptional courage since for years the country had submitted to Guzman's every whim and they still feared that he might regain power. There were open attacks against Guzman's administration and they denounced all his acquisitions of great wealth and onerous contracts. It needed courage to deride him, for everyone was well aware that from the President downward, no mercy could be expected at his hands. Nevertheless Andral believed that Rojas Paul was prepared for all eventualities. On 28 October the statues of Guzman and his father were pulled down. This popular feeling was headed by university students. Andral commented on the fact that he could only wonder at the order and moderation displayed throughout by 5,000 men or more bent upon retaliation for past sufferings.

On 29 October, Guzman's resignation was accepted. On 18 June Reddan had written to Jervoise of the Foreign Office apprising him of the resignation of former ministers and friends of Guzman Blanco; there was even news that the opponents of Guzman had been appointed to public offices. But there were also rumours of revolutionary intrigues led by Guzman's friends in Trinidad. This would have repercussions on Anglo-Venezuelan relations. The Venezuelan Government would once more be bedevilled with the fear of a revolutionary revolt sprung from Trinidad, and Trinidad would be beset by the complications arising from the presence of Venezuelan would-be rebels.

At this time Crespo, remembering Rojas Paul's generosity in releasing him from prison after his abortive revolt, returned to Venezuela and offered his services to the President, while publicly denouncing Guzman Blanco. Guzman's candidate and party for the presidency was withdrawn from the contest and support for him ceased to exist. There was a general wish for Rojas Paul to continue in office, and offer himself as candidate for he had the support of the country. The country had been too long in the pernicious power of Guzman. Now, despite the popular tumult against him, Guzman could not believe the country had turned against him even though his party accepted this fact.

What impact, if any, did Rojas Paul's brief administration have on the country? First of all he attempted to govern generously and 'to preserve public peace and the exercise of orderly liberty I shall omit no means'. Unlike Guzman, however, he believed in magnanimity, e.g. the release of Crespo and fellow rebels. He himself summed up the course of his administration as 'peace, legality, concord, firm dignity in home relations as well as in foreign relations; railways, encouragement to our national industries, special interest in the prosperity of the States, and integrity in all its branches'. Indeed, if all these aspirations had been successfully carried out by Rojas Paul and his successors, Venezuela would not have fallen into economic chaos, nor would Castro and the Andinos have kept their relentless grip on the country destroying all semblance of democracy. What Rojas Paul did realise was the importance of civic rule in Venezuela as opposed to either military dictatorship or chaos from which the country had suffered far too long. But the disastrous two-year presidency term of office was far too short a period to enable him to establish any lasting benefits on the country, and his successors did little to follow in his footsteps. This again was to affect Anglo-Venezuelan relations and be a contributing factor towards the Anglo-German blockade.

Regarding his foreign policy, Rojas Paul pledged himself to defend Venezuela's claims in the boundary question, and in this he was the spokesman of his country's aspirations. The other factor gravely affecting Anglo-Venezuelan relations was the continued imposition of the differential duties. These duties had originated with Guzman Blanco in 1881 as a retaliatory measure against Trinidad for having resisted all his attempts to produce the surrender of his political opponents who had taken refuge on that island. Though this was certainly true, it would not be forgotten that any Venezuelan Government when faced with the threat of a revolution sprung from near-by Trinidad was without doubt terrified at the prospect of civil war. Therefore fear was to a great extent one of the mainsprings for any measures taken against Trinidad. The differential duties had far-reaching economic repercussions. It meant encouragement to German and American trade to the detriment of British merchants in British colonies and assisted illegitimate trade with increased smuggling. This factor is reflected in Trinidad's report on *Our Trade with Venezuela*. The fact that Rojas Paul did nothing to remove the duty, confirmed the continuity of Venezuela's foreign policy with Great Britain as regards Trinidad, as also his policy regarding the boundary question. Both these facts represented fundamental issues to Venezuela. The continuity of this policy by all Venezuela's presidents proves the importance of these two issues in Venezuelan eyes.

On the home front, perhaps Rojas Paul's biggest contribution was his restoration of constitutional rights. The result was to make Guzman's former tyranny so hateful that any reactionary movement by Guzman Blanco's followers was to prove completely impotent. When Rojas Paul left the presidency, he was respected for his energy and republican virtues, his impartiality and devotion to the public services. He encouraged the commerce of foreign nations, as well as that of agriculture, and since there was peace, progress could take place. There was also a rapprochement with the U.S. during these critical years. The settlement and payment of the American claims, the result of the Pan American Congress, made relations between the U.S. and Venezuela more amicable and close. The fact that the administration of Rojas Paul inspired confidence meant that the U.S. would receive great benefits as she was Venezuela's natural market.

The presidential election took place on 7 March 1890 and resulted in the choice of Dr Raimundo Andueza Palacio. Although this was somewhat surprising, as it was generally believed that Rojas Paul, the acting president, would be the successful candidate, the news of the election was received with much pleasure by the Venezuelans in New York. They concurred in the opinion that it meant the continuance of Rojas Paul's policy. In this administration Andueza Palacio had served as Minister of the Interior. It also meant uninterrupted opposition to Guzman Blanco.

The new president of Venezuela was forty-seven years old when he took office. He had studied law and political economy. Besides having been Minister of the Interior, he had also held the portfolios of foreign affairs and of finance, having several times been a member of the Federal Council, and he was considered among the best journalists of Venezuela. By rights therefore Venezuela faced a happier future than had hitherto been her lot. Since Rojas Paul resigned the presidency at the close of his term of office, Andueza Palacio could be elected constitutionally. And this election was probably the first that ever occurred in Venezuela within the proper limits of time, and in due accordance with the law. The constitutional practice was that the new President should be elected in the first and third year of each congress. It should now be noted that Andueza Palacio came into office as an exponent of legal practices which made it even more tragic for Venezuela, in view of what happened at the end of his presidential term. But meanwhile all augured well for Venezuela, as Andueza Palacio was also greatly esteemed by the business profession.

The inauguration of the new President was not only popular in official circles, but also with the journals of Caracas and they expressed great hopes that the country would make rapid progress under his rule. The discourse of the new President addressed to congress on his inauguration expressed the high ideals of liberty and progress but he denounced Britain as an aggressive invader with respect to the Guyana territory. It appeared to British officials, as well as the press, that the Venezuelans were making very heavy weather and they deplored Venezuela's attitude. Nevertheless a section of the British press as well as British commercial houses whose interests were affected by the present unsatisfactory state of affairs, tried to bring pressure to bear on the Foreign Office. What the British failed to realise was the intensity of feeling with which this matter was viewed in Venezuela, and even though as a politician Andueza Palacio later acted in a spirit contrary to his fiery words, at his inauguration he could have hardly spoken differently.[1]

Since the boundary question loomed large for Venezuela, it was logical that Andueza Palacio should take the necessary steps to try and come to a settlement with the British Government, as it gravely affected Anglo-Venezuelan relations. As early as 5 July 1890 a special envoy, Señor L. Pulido, was sent to treat with the Foreign Office, and it was remarked that

---

[1] *South American Journal*, 31 May 1890. Extract from a private letter from Venezuela: 'the boundary question with British Guiana is similar to the intensity of feeling created by the Portuguese African imbroglio with Portugal'.

the South American section of the London Chamber of Commerce proposed that a committee should be formed to bring about a friendly influence on the British Government in order, if possible, to hasten a settlement.[1]

It had been in 1884 that Guzman Blanco, then Venezuelan Minister Plenipotentiary in Europe, had begun negotiations with Lord Granville regarding the boundary dispute, and an attempt was made to establish the basis for a treaty. But as Guzman always considered his personal interest before those of his country, he lost precious time in covetous haggling. With the fall of the Gladstone ministry, the Marquis of Salisbury took office. Salisbury closed all discussion, and it was he who decided upon the occupation of the territory in dispute in 1884, thus consummating the first act of violent usurpation. Guzman Blanco was certainly to blame for not having taken advantage of Granville's proposals; but bent as usual on making money, he insisted on payment by Great Britain of £1,000,000 in consideration of a rectification of the boundaries as marked on a British geographical map. Salisbury's reply was that Britain did not purchase lands, but occupied those which she held to be necessary. When the British made an ostentatious show of occupying Venezuelan territory in 1887 (perhaps intending to provoke explanations with a view to arriving at an arrangement) Guzman Blanco suddenly put an end to diplomatic relations with Great

---

[1] *South American Journal*, 5 July 1890. Facts relating to the dispute: Up to 1884 the question of the boundary between Venezuela and British Guiana although unsettled did not cause too much trouble although Venezuela had always reiterated her claim. By the treaty of 1850 a strip of territory between the two countries was considered neutral; it was understood that neither party was to occupy it. But in 1884 the British Government, having heard that Venezuela had granted a concession of lands in this district to some United States citizens, took official possession of the whole territory by proclamation issued by the Governor of British Guiana. Immediately upon this being announced, the Venezuelan Government cancelled the concession which had been granted, upon the grounds that the concessionaire had not complied with the stipulations of the law, and they also requested Britain to withdraw from the position it had taken. Notwithstanding this, Britain still maintained its claim to the territory and adhered to its nominal occupation.

Britain. This rude proceeding deprived Venezuela of the inter-vention of friendly nations in its support. It was the opinion of many Venezuelans that Guzman Blanco was to a large extent to blame for the unsatisfactory relations between Great Britain and Venezuela.

As regards Andueza Palacio's envoy to Britain, the agent first went to Paris to confer with Guzman Blanco, instead of going to England to treat with the Foreign Office. The result was that he then proceeded to the United States to solicit 'the benevolent intervention of Mr Secretary Blaine'. This action caused the United States to be deliberately involved in the dispute. Pulido, the envoy, was very well received by President Harrison and Secretary Blaine and they both expressed to him their great interest in his mission. It was noted that the United States was paying special attention to South American affairs. In view of the importance of the Orinoco River and its tribu-taries the United States could only disapprove of its estuary being controlled by any European nation and they hoped the affair would be successfully resolved.

By 29 November 1890 Andueza Palacio was making his own position clear. General Level de Goda, President of the Con-gress, was travelling in Europe. He stated that he would use his influence in Venezuela to bring about a settlement of the un-fortunate territorial dispute, and he also declared that Andueza Palacio did not support the position taken by Guzman Blanco, one which practically closed the door to arbitration. It was hoped that there would be an end to the quarrel which, if pro-longed, could endanger the commercial relations of England and Venezuela. This would be to the manifest advantage of other nations such as Germany and the United States, each competing with Britain for the supply of the Venezuelan market and the general opening up of the interior, with its rich mineral and agricultural resources. The one drawback was the unsettled boundary dispute, for while it continued to drag on, British enterprise in all that region suffered, for capital is sensitive to such influences.

Thus the presidency of Andueza Palacio proved a great disappointment from the domestic and foreign point of view, and the boundary dispute remained a burning issue, at any rate as far as Venezuela was concerned, for there was an interruption of negotiations. From the domestic point of view the unfortunate Venezuela jumped from the frying pan into the fire. In the second year of his tenure of power Andueza Palacio's friends began to agitate for a change in the constitution which should permit the retention of office for another two years, making the presidential term four years instead of two. This proposal was unacceptable to a very large majority of the republic. But as the time for re-election approached Dr Andueza Palacio threw off the mask of legality he had worn at the start of his presidency, and put himself at the head of the agitators, refusing to call congress together, and thus forcibly violating the constitution in order to maintain his position as President in the face of every risk and opposition. Crespo, twice disappointed of the high office of President, regarded the action of Andueza Palacio as a usurpation, which stopped him from the enjoyment of what he considered his moral rights. Civil protests being of no avail, Crespo appealed to arms. The struggle for supremacy was severe for 'Venezuelans were good fighters and cruel barbarian soldiers' and with this state of lawlessness British interests suffered immensely.

When Andueza Palacio had taken office he had been a man of limited means, but it was rumoured that when he left Venezuela he took with him a very considerable amount of money (£500,000 sterling clandestinely remitted to Paris before he fled the country) besides the enormous sum said to have been transmitted to London and stated to be lodged at Baring. In Venezuela the funds which should have been found in the National Treasury were discovered to be deficient by 17,000,000 Bolivares, about £680,000 in addition to the cost of fighting the revolution. Thus, besides his unhappy and unlawful policy, Andueza Palacio left his country saddled with even greater debts.

Once more the old pattern of bloodshed, military operations and conflicts was being repeated. Andueza Palacio had been elected with high hopes for the continuation of legal and civil rule, but the perennial struggle to grasp the supreme power prevailed. When he was finally forced to flee from the troubles which he had created or exacerbated, he left behind Villegas, an incompetent. This was to Crespo's advantage for he was the up and coming man. But these violent domestic troubles were already having repercussions on foreign relations for the lives and properties of foreigners, as well as those of the natives, were at stake. It was also a serious matter for the commercial community for besides their obvious losses, they were called upon to maintain the troops. In the consular district of Ciudad Bolivar, the situation for British subjects was critical, for there were large numbers of British subjects in the mining district where vast amounts of British capital were invested.

By June the situation was disastrous, for the revolutionary movement had spread throughout the country and the severe encounters resulted in considerable loss of life. On the whole it could be said that the revolutionary movement was popular, but the chief victim was the country itself. Both parties recruited from the agricultural labourers, another reason for the disastrous economic condition, for the rainy season could not be taken advantage of to sow maize, beans, weeding of coffee trees, etc. All this helped Crespo in his rise to power, but above all it laid the conditions for making the Andinos politically ambitious, with such tragic results for the country. The scarcity of food weighed heavily on the lower classes, and the planters were unable to meet their liabilities. As it was the merchants and shopkeepers had difficulty in keeping their heads above water. Transactions were practically nil, counter orders were sent to restrain the shipping of merchandise. There was even considerable difficulty in cashing notes of the Bank of Venezuela, and there was a daily rise in the price of beef and vegetables. 'A tragedy for this so lately prosperous country.'

With Andueza Palacio's flight and the incompetent Guillermo

Tel Villegas left to take charge of the executive, all was nearly over bar the shouting. Political prisoners were released and he called on members of the late congress to meet and elect a president. The constitution was to be revised and discussed, which was exactly the point which had caused the loss of lives of thousands, and had resulted in such a lamentable state of the country. Commissions were sent to Crespo, head of the revolution. But before his final triumph the worst fears were confirmed as regards fighting and the economic situation. Crespo's triumph, and later disastrous economic position is explained by the course of these events, in the fact that forced loans were levied. Finally Dr Guillermo Tel Villegas, whose crass ineptitude had distinguished him, embarked for New York with his accomplices, leaving behind him an unendurable situation. Many of the principal native merchants and private individuals were imprisoned though few foreigners were attacked because of the Diplomatic Corps' vigorous action and the presence of men-of-war at La Guaira.

The strong man left in Caracas was General Luciano Mendoza, who now assumed the presidency without the right to do so. But revolutionary forces were marching on Caracas and it was whispered that Mendoza would be leaving with goodly sums which he had extorted from the inhabitants whom he was supposed to be protecting. It was not till 7 October, however, that Crespo entered Caracas, and on 10 October he assumed the reins of government. As provisional President of the republic he named a ministry composed of respectable men, causing great satisfaction. The most important and beneficial result was that confidence was restored. Business improved and the disbandment of forces provided the essential labour to save the abundant coffee crop.

Crespo's proclamation promised to restore order and re-organise the country morally and politically. Crespo had been a good fighter, but he was overfond of power. He felt he had been cheated of the presidency by Andueza, whose high office he had coveted. The long struggle for supremacy which he eventually achieved with so much bloodshed, was marred and tainted by the fatal flaw of ambition as his only apparent motive. And this was hardly worthy of the great loss of life and frightful devastation which the war had exacted. One final thing should be noted. It is significant that both Cipriano Castro and Juan Vicente Gomez, the two future Andean presidents who perpetrated their rule, backed Andueza Palacio in his struggle to remain in power illegally.

But behind the façade of Andueza's fight to remain in office, the Foreign Office thought that the sinister figure of Guzman Blanco could be detected lurking in the background. According to Reddan, Andueza had tried to prolong his presidency because of the intrigues of Guzman and his party, who had been taking measures for this purpose a long time: 'Il paraît que le diable n'est pas encore mort'. But despite these intrigues, Guzman's power was on the wane and the Convention authorised Crespo's continuance in office as head of the executive until the election of a constitutional president in 1894. Furthermore, that body had sanctioned all his acts and proceedings during and since the revolution.

It was Crespo's policy to reinforce his role as national leader and affirm his country's sovereignty for this strengthened his position at home. He therefore declared that foreigners had equal rights with natives and were to be treated in the same way for 'Venezuela neither does nor will recognise other obligations and responsibilities in favour of foreigners than those enjoyed by natives.' It was the affirmation of a small weak nation against the powerful great powers.[1] He decreed that foreigners who had been six months in the country as well as new arrivals should state their birthplace, last domicile, profession, means of subsistence, name, age, nationality of wife and children under age. This was much objected to, but the Foreign Office com-

[1] The sovereignty of the nation was an important and popular issue. See also Andral—Salisbury, 8 November 1895, No. 22, Political F.O. 80/359. Aggressive acts by great powers were considered by the Venezuelan press as a slight to the country and the people who 'were violent where honour is concerned'. This is reminiscent of some of the smaller new nations of today!

mented that no one could take exception though undoubtedly it was vexatious. The Diplomatic Corps could not intervene in an internal policy which appeared to be directed against the admission of undesirable aliens. Yet the reasonableness of Crespo's policy did not obscure the fact that it was the protest of the weak against the powerful nations who dominated her economically, and above all it was extremely popular domestically.

As regards Venezuela's attitude towards the United Kingdom, diplomatic relations had been suspended on 21 March 1887 and had not yet been resumed, for the British Government did not consider it necessary to make a special representation to General Crespo. From Venezuela's point of view Crespo's presidential term of office marked the apex of a 'freeze-up' both officially and unofficially. What emerges clearly are two facts, the weakness of Venezuela's internal condition, and at the same time her almost aggressive attitude towards the great European powers. This was especially so regarding the United Kingdom for with her she asserted her natural sovereignty and territorial integrity.

First of all it is important to realise how disastrous Venezuela's domestic condition was for it had a decided effect on her policy. The political outlook, Reddan wrote to the Foreign Office, was far from reassuring two years after Crespo's rise to power. For all his promises, he was marching along the same road as his predecessor. In the matter of filling his own pocket, he had taken his old chief Guzman Blanco as his model; so faithfully was he following the example of Venezuela's former ruler, that he bid fair to rival his spoils. There was growing discontent in all parts of the country, and great dissatisfaction with the acts of the Government, powerful factors which in themselves were to contribute towards Castro's and the Andinos' rise to power.

As regards Crespo's financial policy, it was a complete failure. In fact a number of ministers who disapproved of it resigned. The Acting British Consul in Caracas, Andral, was well aware of this and also of the bad effect it had on Venezuelan

trade. Accordingly in his report on Trade and Finance to the
Foreign Office for 1895, he pointed out the defects and failures
that had taken place. He also noted that owing to political considerations, it was expected that trade between the United
States and Venezuela would show a marked increase; and a
great incentive to this end was the facility of communication,
and the proximity of the countries. This then is an instance of
Venezuela's domestic policy having repercussions on Anglo-
American relations. A further point should be noted, that this
report provoked an attack on Andral in one of the daily papers
of Caracas, *El Noticiero* of 11 June 1896, 'as the editor considered it offensive towards the society in which I have lived
for many years'. But the Foreign Office believed the attack
quite unjustified, and once more this incident only served to
sour relations between the two countries.

Yet despite this prevalent attitude the republic still offered
sufficient inducements for capital and enterprise, for its rich and
varied interior was destitute of good roads and other means of
communication to its seaboard. Most of the excellent railways
and public works were built with British capital, e.g. the
Quebrada Land, Railway & Mining Company Ltd owned the
railway from the sea-board of Tucacas to the copper mines at
Aroa. The La Guaira & Caracas Railway was built with British
money, aided by a subsidy from the State. This line, forming the
means of communication from the capital of the republic and
its chief sea-port, was a great success. The Puerto Cabello &
Valencia Railway, uniting Valencia with its sea outlet, the
natural harbour of Puerto Cabello, was constructed entirely
with British capital with the advantage of a guarantee from the
Government. But in many of these financial enterprises the
'crisis of affairs between Venezuela and Britain' had a direct
impact on these financial ventures, so that in 1897 Andral could
write to Salisbury that the hopes which had been cherished by
those interested in the commerce and agriculture of Venezuela
at the beginning of 1896 had not been realised.

One of the main reasons was the failure of the coffee crop of

1896, but the principal difficulty in the way of trade was because there was no increase in the demand owing to the almost stationary condition of the population. Besides this there were few, if any, lucrative industries, necessitating retrenchment on the part of the consumers. German trade however had increased, to the detriment of British commerce. In Andral's opinion this was due mainly to the fact that the British paid very little attention to Venezuela and did little to promote business relations with the Republic. On the other hand, Germans attained their favourable position through steady perseverance; they ingratiated themselves with the natives of their adopted home and acquired the language quickly and thoroughly, thus gaining the sympathy of the Venezuelan people. The largest firms in Venezuela were German, but there was not a single British firm in Venezuela.

In Crespo's favour it may be said that he had inherited a very heavy burden. Not least were the instances of breach of faith by Guzman Blanco, an onerous patrimony indeed. In all fairness, responsible men in Venezuela were fully aware of the necessity of tackling Venezuela's financial problems at the very roots. Therefore a settlement of the unification of the debt had to be reached. Indeed an article in a leading newspaper *El Tiempo* headed 'The Public Debt of Venezuela' pointed out the dangers inherent in this situation. 'It is imperative that this problem be solved', they wrote.

First, these financial problems must also be seen against Venezuela's own domestic background. As has been noted, a very bitter feeling existed against Britain, due in great part to the passions aroused by the territorial dispute over British Guiana. Venezuela, the much weaker country, felt she had been deprived of her territorial integrity, and no amount of legal quibbling or words could soften the blow to her injured pride. This was an aspect all too easily ignored in Britain, but acknowledged by those who had lived in Venezuela. At that date Britain's consul was H. L. Boulton, junior partner to the firm of that name. Mr Middleton (formerly Resident British Minister in

Caracas) had pointed out that British commerce suffered also from the fact that Messrs Boulton's business connections were almost exclusively limited to the United States. Also in the chief towns and ports of Venezuela, such as La Guaira, Puerto Cabello and Maracaibo, all the vice-consuls worked for the affiliated firms of Boultons. Thus the interests of the firm were clearly to promote trade with the U.S.A., and the existence of the 30 per cent upon the shipments from the West Indies was entirely in their favour. And as seen, there were no longer any British firms at Caracas, for their place was taken by two large German houses and smaller ones too. In every way it was a period of growth of German interests.

On Thursday 12 March 1896, the President's message to Congress was published, which illustrates perfectly the extent to which Venezuela was becoming more and more indebted to Imperial Germany in the economic field. This was for Venezuela a matter of the 'highest transcendency for the dominions'. At that date Crespo presented to the legislators a plan to save the Republic from the pernicious 7 per cent security, which had to be suppressed in railway contracts. The position as regards Venezuela was as follows. The Treasury was unable to meet her contracted engagements, which could only go on increasing in an astounding manner. This was an evil, Venezuela realised, which had to be destroyed. The national Government had to draw out 3 million Bolivares annually, for interest and amortisation of the loan, from the customs unities allotted for this purpose. The President's message spoke of the unities of the National Revenue, and as there entered into this accounts which were not customs' returns, *El Tiempo* considered that it was a point which had to be clearly explained in the definitive contract, *in order to avoid* future conflicts. Thus if Venezuela's rulers did not foresee the pitfalls there is little doubt that the more serious section of the population were very much aware of the dangers inherent in such a situation. In other words it was essential that everything that could assure the payment of the debt, would insure the credit.

At that time railways were a powerful means for the development and agriculture industry of the country. But the 7 per cent security in the contracts with various undertakings which profited from Venezuela's needs, placed a very heavy burden upon the nation with the increased sums that for a series of years would have to be disbursed, and for the payments of which it would be necessary to augment the sources of the national income. In effect, for the building and maintenance of the railways that had been contracted for, it would be necessary to expend large sums in gold annually, for a series of years. This would be the equivalent to continuing to allow the disbursement to go on increasing annually, and to have two indefinite obligations to meet instead of one: that of the 7 per cent on the capital guaranteed, and that of the interest and amortisation of the bonds emitted, and which would probably have to be continued every year.

Because of this, Crespo considered it more convenient for the Government and for the railways to liquidate by means of an equitable indemnity the obligation of continuing to pay in future during the entire period of the ninety-nine years stipulated in the contracts. The Minister of Public Works was therefore authorised to negotiate with the railway companies. In order to carry out his plan Crespo had to obtain the money from a first class banking institute. He therefore entered into negotiations with the directors of the Disconto Gesellschaft of Berlin. The Disconto agreed on a loan of 50,000,000 Bolivares at the rate of 80 per cent by means of an emission of stock with 5 per cent interest annually, and 1 per cent for amortisation also annually, which was equivalent to cancelling the said amount in thirty-six and a half years. This issue the Bank would make itself with the security of the Government of Venezuela, represented in unities of the national revenue sufficient to cover the sum of 3 million Bolivares annually and the amortisation of the capital.

From the British point of view the situation was far from satisfactory. In a confidential letter to Mr Campbell of the

Foreign Office, Reddan wrote that Venezuela was virtually bankrupt, and at any moment could be declared so openly. The German Disconto Gesellschaft, as seen, were creditors to the tune of 50,000,000 francs, at a very high rate of interest. For this loan they held a guarantee of the revenues from imports and exports. But if matters came to a head the Germans would without doubt put forward a preferential claim to all the other powers holding recognised claims against the Venezuelan government. *Ipso facto* the republic would be wholly unable to meet all its engagements.

Over and above the economic situation in Venezuela, there was the accumulation of circumstances militating against England such as the territorial dispute which had been the direct cause of broken diplomatic relations, with the result that, as seen, British interests had suffered badly. Both Americans and Germans could take advantage of their favourable circumstances to the detriment of the British.

Although relations dropped to their lowest pitch during Crespo's presidency, paradoxically new hope dawned and attempts were made for a friendly and equitable settlement of the questions at issue between the two countries, so that a new and special representation could be made to Crespo on the subject. Unfortunately all these high hopes proved abortive and Crespo's presidency is marked by the iciest of relations reached between Venezuela and Great Britain. 'Under his administration relations reached an icy pitch.'[1]

From the international point of view, the boundary dispute is important in that it crystallised Anglo-American relations. It may be said that for Great Britain it was the moment of truth as regards her attitude towards the United States, though obviously the process had been at work for a number of years. Other, earlier issues, much more important to her, had a great impact

[1] Bradford Perkins, p. 26. 'The Venezuelan imbroglio not only overshadowed all the other issues during Cleveland's last year in the White House, they also influenced lesser matters, including an effort to carry through an Anglo-American arbitration Treaty . . . soon the Venezuelan controversy arose to cast a pall over the project.'

on Anglo-American relations. Thus however unimportant and insignificant the issue is made out to be from the British point of view, it played its part in the retrenchment in the Caribbean and in the international game of world politics.

Since it is not the present object to deal with the boundary dispute but only note the impact it had on Anglo-Venezuelan relations, it is important to establish the fact that the issue was forced on Great Britain because the Americans wanted it to be settled, and because of this it affected Anglo-American relations. The English publicist William T. Stead argued that Venezuela proved the danger of 'rubbing along, taking no thought as to the morrow, and trusting that whenever a difficulty or a hitch arose, the two nations would be able to impose a way out'.

Perhaps the best way it was forced on Great Britain as an issue is a commentary from the *Commercial Gazette*: 'all nations in Christendom have been startled by the possibility of a war between Great Britain and the United States. The situation is simply this: in pursuance of well settled policy of the United States, supported with unanimity by the people, and not dependent upon its relation to international law nor any definition of the Monroe Doctrine, Britain is practically called upon to show the ground of what appears strongly to us as an unwarranted assumption and aggression in conflict with this settled policy, and which if found to be so this government cannot tolerate.' Another newspaper, the *New York Herald*,[1] also put forward the view of the United States and it was this aspect of the dispute which carried weight in Great Britain.

For the United States the issue tended to rouse emotions, as to a great many Americans the phrase 'Monroe Doctrine' had a magic charm. Without enquiring into its historic meaning and its applicability to the Venezuelan case, it was rather a sentiment than a doctrine, all the more seductive as it was vague. A

[1] The *New York Herald*, 25 April 1894: 'Great Britain in violation of the Monroe Doctrine and without any authority . . . has taken possession of a great part of the republic of Venezuela, and is building a line of fortification at the mouth of the river Orinoco.'

British correspondent, a fur trader by profession, explained the situation and its inherent dangers very clearly to H.M.'s Government: 'I do not presume to offer any opinion', he wrote, 'but there is one point the correspondent has not exaggerated . . . that is the feeling in the United States regarding the Monroe Doctrine. History does not make the slightest difference . . . they do not care anything about what was . . . the interpretation is all they care about. As a Canadian I feel that what is not claimed today will be claimed tomorrow, that now the merits of the Venezuelan affair are secondary. The undefined doctrine will be made to do duty and stretched in any shape, in the various questions which must necessarily arise in consequence of the position of Canada. That President Cleveland has created the unrecognised Monroe Doctrine as the main question . . . that it will be necessary in the interests of peace between the two nations for the United States and the United Kingdom to agree on a definition of the Monroe Doctrine . . . and to confirm it by treaty. This was the only way out of further complications especially with regard to Canada.' *This* was the importance of the dispute to the United Kingdom. Venezuela was too small and too weak to have any real impact. For Britain the issue was only important in that it had an impact on Anglo-American relations. But for Venezuela it was a very different matter. The young republic seethed under the lash of Britain's disdain and struggled unsuccessfully to assert her claims to what she considered her lost national territory. Under Crespo's presidency, the quarrel reached one of its bitterest peaks, and the impact of the quarrel was yet another factor which soured Anglo-Venezuelan relations. Last but not least, Venezuela was only too aware of the dangers inherent in the intervention by the United States on her behalf. 'If the Monroe Doctrine is converted by the Cabinet at Washington into a leadership over our weak governments, we will save a part of Guyana; but we will have met with the "carbine of Ambrosis" (said of useless things)'. This prophetic remark was fulfilled at the aftermath of the Anglo-German blockade.

Besides these two crushing burdens, the disastrous financial policy and the boundary question which Crespo faced, he also had to cope with the perennial problems posed by Trinidad. There were the usual revolutionary attempts organised from Trinidad to overthrow Venezuelan governments, and the corresponding smuggling of arms and ammunition. Crespo repeatedly warned the Governor of Trinidad that the introduction of arms into Venezuela by would-be revolutionists would threaten the country's peace, and as a result relations between the colony and Venezuela could not improve. This made the task of the Imperial Government even harder.

Eventually diplomatic relations were resumed and the new Resident British Minister, W. H. D. Haggard, wrote from Caracas to the Foreign Office, announcing his arrival and the fact that he had taken possession of H.M.'s Legation. Haggard's appointment, however, was to prove a most unhappy choice, for his obvious antipathy towards Venezuela and her people, as well as his complete lack of understanding, is apparent from his earliest despatches. This antipathy was later to tilt the balance against Venezuela, and become a contributing factor resulting in the Anglo-German blockade.

Some time after taking up office as Resident Minister, Haggard became only too aware of Germany's energetic, forceful, if menacing attitude towards Venezuela. He realised too that the German clashes with the Venezuelan Government did not bid well for the future.[1] Germany's indifference to the Monroe

---

[1] Haggard—Salisbury, 2 February 1898, No. 13, Confidential F.O. 80/385: 'Count Rex . . . has demanded and received an undertaking in writing.' Haggard—Salisbury, 8 February 1898, No. 18, Confidential F.O. 80/385. Also Haggard—Salisbury, 9 February 1898, No. 19, Confidential F.O. 80/385: 'the British are afraid they won't be paid if Germans paid. U.S. and Germany find it necessary to use menaces to make rights respected and debts paid.' Note how Haggard, even at this early stage as Minister, is continually reiterating the efficacy of the use of force. See also Haggard—Salisbury, 3 December 1897, F.O. 80/377. Note the importance of *Germany*, her great commerce, her use of force, her setting aside, or ignoring the Monroe Doctrine. This attitude would be important prior to Anglo-German blockade. Also Haggard—Salisbury, 15 December, 1897, F.O. 80/377. The importance of *Germany* in the New

Doctrine might possibly take her a step further should occasion arise, particularly in view of the Kaiser's exaggerated protection of German interests in Latin America. Fears and doubts were therefore raised in the minds of the American people. In the eyes of most Latin Americans, however, the result of brute force could only have one sequel, a much reduced or lost market, and above all a hostile people for there was nothing more unjust than the imposition of humiliation on the weak. Haggard noted the fact that the United States had lately emphasised the dogma of the Monroe Doctrine, particularly with regard to Venezuela. Should the occasion arise, it would therefore be interesting to see how she would meet Germany's total indifference to this policy.[1]

Meanwhile Crespo's term as President was fast drawing to a close, and the impoverished treasury made it impossible for Venezuela to meet her foreign commitments. The fact was that this situation was the result of the wholesale annexation of public money by the President. 'The Treasury was absolutely empty and there is no money forthcoming for any government obligation.' Everything was seized by the President who seemed determined to make hay while the sun shone. He 'borrowed' large sums estimated at $2 million from all sorts of business houses who did not dare resist his demands though they knew they would probably never see their money again. In his vivid but verbose style Haggard's despatches give an excellent picture of the political complications which arose. As the

---

World. Germany had great commercial stakes in Venezuela and the enterprise which she displays in Venezuela is remarkable. An interesting and almost prophetic despatch. See also Haggard–Salisbury, 13 January 1898, No. 7, Secret, F.O. 80/385. The German Minister said: 'Nous nous fichons pas mal de la Doctrine Monroe' which illustrates bullying tactics of Germany against Venezuela.

[1] The United States would later bring all possible pressure to bear on the United Kingdom during the Anglo-German blockade, 1902–3, in order to make her part company with her German ally. Without doubt this further affected Anglo–American relations.

moment approached for Crespo to resign office, the problems of the future became more and more apparent. It was generally thought that Crespo would protect his nominee—General Ignacio Andrade—against all comers. Andrade himself was thought little of.

Though Crespo was willing to back him, nevertheless he was not eager to abandon power. In this he resembled his former master Guzman Blanco. Crespo seemed determined to continue to be the real ruler of the country and dictate his will to Andrade either in matters connected with his own private interests or with those of the republic. Faced with this twofold difficulty of defending and commanding Andrade, Crespo established an armed camp at Maracay, in the State of Miranda, where he had been appointed President. Maracay was within a few days' march of Caracas or five hours by railway, near enough for Crespo to influence events according to his liking. Haggard believed that if Andrade acquiesced to Crespo's rule, public order might not be disturbed, but if he opposed it actively Crespo would overthrow him unless Andrade resisted by force of arms. It was generally thought that Andrade would not accept Crespo's domination longer than was necessary. Therefore there was a very real possibility of another civil war looming on the horizon. While in power Crespo had amassed an enormous fortune and now disposed of a considerable part of the army. But Andrade on the other hand enjoyed the advantages of being the man in possession. Should a civil war be avoided Haggard believed that the two men would continue to rob the treasury so that the immediate future for the unfortunate Venezuela was not very bright, particularly as she also had to face foreign complications as a result of non-payment of debts.

There was a further entanglement to this unhappy situation: this was the threat that Guzman Blanco himself might return to Venezuela in a last bid as President. His followers were flocking back, and sufficient time had elapsed for people to have forgotten Guzman's misdeeds. They only remembered the wealth and the luxury which they had enjoyed under his rule. In contrast, Crespo's presidency had been marked by anarchy and poverty. With the advent of Andrade's administration, Guzman Blanco's brother-in-law, Matos, was the most important man in the new administration. Because of the precarious state of the country, politically and financially, Haggard thought that British capitalists should bide their time before further investments in Venezuela.

Andrade's election had been suspect, and this of course was the main reason for his indebtedness to Crespo with all its inherent dangers. Another result of this jerrymandered election was the frustration and fury of the defeated candidate José Manuel Hernandez (El Mocho). El Mocho is one of the most romantic figures in Venezuelan history, and also a tragic one for by his fantastic charm he ensnared large numbers, leading them to a seemingly never-ending series of civil wars. Furious at his defeat by Andrade, El Mocho left Caracas in order to raise the flag of revolt against the new administration. By 5 March, Haggard was already informing Salisbury that as a prompt sequel to Andrade's inauguration a revolution had broken out led by General Hernandez, who seemed to lack money and troops. It was imperative for Andrade to suppress it immediately, otherwise the financial future looked desperately gloomy. It meant that foreign countries had little chance of being paid interest on the debt, and payments on claims would not be met.[1] There were even rumours that unless the revolution was at an end very shortly, a motion should be brought forward in Congress to suppress the payment of the interest on foreign debts.

[1] Haggard—Salisbury, 2 April 1898, No. 47, Confidential F.O. 80/385. Andrade's Minister of Finance, however, seemed well disposed towards British demands and said that if he could prevent it the German Disconto Gesellschaft would have no preference given over the British debt. Said the revolution had affected them badly. American Minister believed the Germans might seize Custom Houses if their coupons were unpaid. According to the United States Minister this did not conflict with the Monroe Doctrine. This was typical of the use of force by the great powers against small defaulting nations.

As far as the domestic situation was affected, men were being impressed in all directions so that there was no labour left to gather in the coffee crop. Crespo was in charge of government troops and it was thought that this in itself was even more dangerous to the State than the revolution itself. Crespo had made large demands on the public purse and as he insisted on being paid in gold it was thought that he kept most of it for himself. This had a twofold result. It was to Crespo's advantage that the revolution should continue, and his unfortunate soldiers were left to forage for themselves. Thus another horror was added to the inevitable evils of civil strife. It was also the general feeling that 'if this goes on long Venezuela is killed . . . and where will she find the money to pay the interest on her foreign debts, and if she does not pay it, what will the Powers then do?'

The stage was being set for the coming of the Andinos, and likewise the (for Venezuela) tragic Anglo-German blockade. Every day it was becoming more obvious that Crespo was an ever-growing danger to the Government, and Matos himself informed Haggard that it had been a great mistake to have appointed Crespo to command the Army. In this same despatch Haggard also reported the rumours flying in Caracas, that a convenient bullet should check a career that was dragging Venezuela to ruin. It was believed too that if Crespo were removed, Hernandez's revolution would *ipso facto* collapse.

By 19 April this death wish had been fulfilled: 'The death of General Crespo', wrote Haggard, 'is most opportune for General Andrade . . . so opportune that it affords the right to every suspicion.' What was important now was that previously Andrade was in a very embarrassing and difficult situation, for he was being driven by his supporters to get rid of Crespo, and was afraid to take the necessary steps to do so. Crespo's death relieved him of immediate action. An opposition paper *El Pregonero* published an article on Crespo's death. 'It should', they wrote, 'make the most incredulous incline to the belief in a Providence which watches over the fate of the country.' There was now every hope that the revolution would come to an end. Yet it was a short-lived hope, for with Crespo's death 'the revolution appeared to have made a fresh start'. Once more Venezuela was going through the usual motions of perennial civil strife, anarchy and poverty.

Chapter 9

❦

Folies de Grandeur

'I was possessed by an overwhelming conviction, stronger than reasoning and will power, that the voice of Destiny, *my Destiny*, was ordering me to put aside a logical course, and to go forward either to victory or death.' Mariano Picon-Salas, 1953, p. 24.

Two aspects of Cipriano Castro, President of Venezuela from 1899 to 1908 and initiator of the emergence and dominance of the Andinos, depict two important traits in his character, both of which were to influence his relations with foreign powers. On the one hand Cipriano Castro deluded himself into believing that he had messianic qualities and that he had been called to 'liberate his People', in brief, to be another Bolivar. 'America', he was wont to exclaim, 'was physically liberated by Bolivar, but nevertheless she continued under Europe's tutelage. I was the one who broke her bonds. I was the one who stood up to England, Germany, Italy and Holland. When they tried to enforce their will, I stood up to them as their equal.'[1] But the fact that Castro triumphed, overthrew President Andrade's Government and seized power was due to a large extent to a cumulation of occurrences throughout the country, all of which contributed to his rise to power and final victory.

It was Venezuela's tragedy that civil strife and unrest should continue to tear the country apart, even after Crespo's death. Haggard himself informed Salisbury that in their consular reports, the British Vice-Consuls at Puerto Cabello and Ciudad Bolivar reiterated that the revolution continued to be very

[1] Mariano Picon-Salas, 1953, p. 25.

active in their districts. The Government took all the usual precautionary methods, which meant that all official business was at a standstill, but 'private ones' flourished with further disastrous economic repercussions to the country's finances. The feeling of confidence and security, which alone could have helped Venezuela at home and abroad, did not exist.

Meanwhile the financial condition of the country seemed to be going from bad to worse. The Venezuelan Minister of Finance reckoned that the receipts would not reach the estimates by one third. In his usual sneering tone Haggard commented that there would be that amount less to be robbed, for Andrade's Government was not less eager to plunder than that of Crespo. Whatever Haggard's tone, however, the sad fact remained that this unbridled system of public theft seriously undermined the country materially and morally.[1] The gravity was that people were so accustomed to these scandals that they excited little comment, and this would also make possible the total acquiescence of the Andinos' corrupt rule, i.e. that of Castro and, later, Gomez.

At one time people had hoped that Andrade might fulfil some of their expectations; he had, however, shown no sign of vigour, resolution and energy by which alone he could restore chaos to order. Even his best friend, such a first-rate one as Santiago Briceño, was writing to him from Tariba that the outlook could not be gloomier.[2] Most foreigners believed that Venezuela was in a worse condition than she had ever been. By

[1] In this same interesting despatch Haggard named the Ministers for Affairs and of Public Credit as having divided 'the spoil' to the amount of 1 million francs 'with one of my colleagues in the recent settlement of some claims'. Thus if Venezuelan Ministers were corrupt, the Diplomatic Corps followed hard on their heels.

[2] The late President Crespo was in power for five years. During that time he amassed a fortune estimated at $15 million a year. It is noteworthy that even such a biased person as was Haggard could add that all Venezuela required to restore its prosperity was a few years of public order and official honesty, for the normal revenue was greatly in excess of the necessary public expenditure. Venezuela could, if she liked, pay off her outstanding claims—and still have funds to develop the great natural resources of the country.

October of that same year, however, Andrade made some attempt to deal with the deteriorating situation. A commission of leading merchants and businessmen was called together with the object of discussing the best means of alleviating the disastrous financial and commercial condition of the country.

From the international point of view, not only did Venezuela's financial situation affect British interests in the country itself, but the republic's precarious monetary problems were a source of concern in that the delicate balance of relations was threatened.

Andrade constantly reiterated that the country's revenue did not meet the expenses of the Government, and though the accuracy of this statement was generally contested, it was now almost universally known that the President was following in his predecessor's footsteps and robbing the country outright.

Haggard was very suspicious of the role which the United States proposed to play regarding Venezuela's financial difficulties. He believed there existed a scheme for raising a loan in the United States. This would consist of a loan to Venezuela of £10 million on the security of the customs, which would be administrated and superintended by United States officials in the interests of the loan. Eight million was to be devoted to the conversion of the public debts of Venezuela. The other 2 million was to be left at the disposal of the Government. Thus the bribe was a heavy one, for in addition to the disposal of the 2 million, the manipulation of the £8 million would give 'some pretty pickings'. There was of course the difficulty of having the loan approved by Congress; the Venezuelans heartily disliked their sovereignty being challenged in this way for they would be bound hand and foot to the United States.[1]

---

[1] See Haggard—Salisbury, No. 132, Confidential, 12 October 1898. F.O. 80/387: The Venezuelans hate the United States 'especially as they think that they have been betrayed by them on the Boundary Arbitration Question, and who would exercise . . . a practical protectorate over the country'. Haggard believed that there was some truth in these rumours because of the American Minister's actions (Mr Loomis) with the Venezuelan Minister of Finance Señor Matos.

It seemed to Haggard that the United States had lately shown a disposition to establish a more tangible hold on the South American republics 'than that afforded by the somewhat vague pretensions of the Monroe Doctrine',[1] while recent events have placed Venezuela geographically still further within the limits of that paramount influence which the United States have lately asserted and 'endeavoured to give effect to'.[2]

[1] But it was not only Haggard who was becoming aware of American interest in the Caribbean: see Playfair, Foreign Office—Chamberlain, Colonial Office, 20 January 1896, J.C. 7/5/1B/19—wherein the importance of the Orinoco is noted as regards the United States. 'This Orinoco fear is deep in the American mind.' The balance of power in the Caribbean economically as well as politically was altering: see Governor Jerningham, Port of Spain, Trinidad—Joseph Chamberlain, Colonial Office, 9 May 1899, C.O./295/392. Also Haggard—Salisbury, No. 82, 14 June 1898, F.O. 80/386. Increased American interest and influence.

[2] Haggard was doubtless referring to American interest in the Guiana boundary question. See also for other instances of American force or threat of force against Venezuela: Haggard—Salisbury, 25 October 1899, F.O. 199/139. Haggard—Salisbury, No. 151, Draft, Confidential, 28 October 1899, F.O. 199–139. Loomis, the American Minister, wished to use force against Venezuela in conjunction with other great powers. As early as 1896 there were British comments regarding U.S. influence in Venezuela. See John Langham Reid —Dr Bruzual Serra, 100 Piccadilly, London, 1 September 1896. J.C. 7/5/B/43: 'The interests of Venezuela are made entirely subservient to the exigencies of politics in the United States. . . . there is a desire to obtain for the U.S. the same kind of influence in South America that England exercises in India . . . England's policy has always been to admit competition, the policy of the United States has always been to exclude competition.' Unofficially, and from their diplomats abroad, the Foreign Office was warned of encroaching American influence. Governor Jerningham, Trinidad—Colonial Office, No. 5471, 3 March 1899, C.O./295/391, and Jerningham—J. Chamberlain, 6 February 1899, C.O./295/391 for U.S. interest in Orinoco. Governor Jerningham was worried over U.S. interest in the Orinoco, but there seems to be some doubt if it was an 'official' American interest, or what at this stage seemed more likely, Mr Loomis' private economic interest in conjunction with that of President Andrade: see Jerningham—Sir Joseph Chamberlain, 20 January 1899, C.O./295/391. Mr Loomis was deeply involved in the Orinoco affair with Andrade. There was another interesting example of American interest in Venezuela—a staff officer Lieutenant Collins was appointed as military attaché at a time when the U.S. needed their military men elsewhere (the Cuban War). Haggard's commentary was that the United States must have considered it important since the U.S. 'had little to learn from the undisciplined ragamuffins which constituted the Venezuelan Army'. See Haggard—Salisbury, 14 June

Should this plan take place, there would be two immediate effects as a result. American influence would predominate and British commercial interests would become less important. On the other hand the peace and quiet which would follow the introduction of a 'quasi' United States Protectorate would add enormously to the country's future receipts. The country's natural resources were boundless and practically untouched due largely to the civil wars which had strangled their development at birth as well as destroying crops, cattle and all property.

Anglo-American relations however were not the only ones which were affected by Venezuela's financial embarrassments. There was the immediate one of the United Kingdom with Venezuela herself, and also those having repercussions on an international basis, such as with Germany and Colombia. On the whole, it could be said that Andrade's attitude was more conciliatory than Crespo's had been. The Minister of Public Credit informed Haggard that the President had instructed him to pay a whole monthly instalment on the debt for that month (October), while next month and from that time forward it was proposed to pay at least 50 per cent of the interest on all foreign debts. More than this would be paid if the state of the revenue permitted.

Crespo had shown a preference for the Germans, but now there appeared to be a reaction.[1] Instead of the Disconto

---

1898, No. 82, F.O. 80/386. Great Britain's official policy was already that of acceptance of American hegemony in the Caribbean: Mr Chamberlain, the Colonial Office informed the Foreign Office, does not think it advisable that any communication on the subject of differential duties should be made to the Government of the United States. See Colonial Office—Foreign Office, Secret draft, 13 March 1899, C.O. 295/391.

[1] See previous chapter for details of the German loan and influence. One important fact should be noted, during the years when diplomatic relations had been broken off between Great Britain and Venezuela. Britain's affairs during these crucial years had been in the hands of the German Legation. There is no doubt that Germany took advantage of her position economically and politically. See Haggard—Campbell of the Foreign Office, 2 July 1898, Private,

Gesellschaft being favoured, the Venezuelans did not intend to make any payment to them until the following month when they would come under the general scheme. Though on the surface Andrade appeared to be much more conciliatory towards Great Britain, his real sympathies were with the United States. Besides, Andrade himself had a personal interest regarding any 'friendly' settlement economically. Thus it can be seen that Venezuela's economic difficulties were affecting their relations with the great powers, as well as creating a feeling of insecurity and frustration within the country. All this was to help Castro in his rise to power, for failure to meet economic commitments with the great powers would inevitably lead to the use of force,[1] or threats of it, with the consequent weakening of the Government's power at home.

President Andrade's weakness in his domestic, economic and foreign policy is clearly reflected in the spate of revolutions which continued to break out spasmodically throughout the country, and which inevitably resulted in Castro's rise to power.

F.O. 80/386. Count Rex's reports from Caracas to Berlin on British affairs were simply 'pigeon-holed'. See also Haggard—Salisbury, No. 153/13, December 1898, F.O. 80/38: Germany did not look after the United Kingdom's interests.

[1] There is little doubt that the dubious methods which the German Legation had used with the Venezuelan Government had left a heritage of trouble for the future. See Haggard—Salisbury, 27 August 1898, No. 117, Confidential, F.O. 80/386: as to the German methods of dealing with the Venezuelan government and the way in which the 'Disconto Gesellschaft' loan was arranged having left behind a heritage of trouble for the German Legation. German bribes were given with Count Rex's (Resident German Minister) knowledge and consent. This meant a loss of prestige for diplomatic envoys and could subsequently interfere with the exercise of legitimate influence of a Legation on behalf of genuine national interests. Haggard predicted this would happen. See Haggard–Salisbury, No. 108, 5 August 1898, F.O. 80/386. Haggard–Salisbury, No. 98, 19 July, F.O. 80/386. The Venezuelan Government was constantly submitted to tremendous German official pressure which weakened Andrade at home and affected his relations with the United Kingdom regarding the republic's debts. See Haggard–Salisbury, No. 130, 2 October 1898, F.O. 80/387.

On 18 May 1898 Haggard was writing to Lord Salisbury that despite Andrade's assurances that the revolution would be all over within three or four days, there was a fight within a few miles of Caracas, followed a few nights afterwards by an attempt to blow up the Federal Palace by a dynamite bomb. On 24 September 1898 Haggard was again reporting 'The suppression of an armed rising in the State of Los Andes and the capture of its leader, General Cardona'. This was quite a distinct movement from the lately suppressed revolution under General Hernandez, a further proof, if proof were needed, of the disorganised state of the country.

Besides the various violent uprisings in nearly every region of the country, Andrade also had to face further trouble in Caracas. The political situation was extremely uncertain. Congress, which met in February, was composed almost entirely of nominees of General Crespo under whose auspices Andrade was himself elected. But as it now appeared that Andrade was showing a tendency to emancipate himself from the trammels in which he was bound by his predecessor, there existed a strong party of malcontents amongst his nominal supporters. Consequently when Congress met, he did not find it the facile tool that Crespo had intended it to be. Andrade now had to counterbalance this expected opposition and provide places for adherents whom he wanted to recompense, or alternatively for opponents whom he wished to conciliate.

However, there were other elements of discord which were quite as dangerous to the peace and security of the country. Venezuela had always been plagued by her bellicose 'caudillos' and at that time they were particularly active. Generals Pulido and Castillo were reported to be organising a revolution and they were consequently imprisoned. In order to understand the full extent of these risings, a brief summary is required.

With the benefit of hindsight, it was a paradox that Andrade, a man from the Andes, should have himself been overthrown by a fellow Andino. However, to some extent Andrade was overthrown because he did little or nothing to remedy the many ills from which his home region was suffering. However, prior to the rise of Cipriano Castro and his fellow Andinos, another group of malcontents formed a party, which was formed by those who were not incorporated in Crespo's ranks (known as Godos or Conservatives). The new party called themselves Nationalists, or Liberal Nationalists, in preference to the term Conservatives, never very popular in Venezuela. Backed by a powerful group of politicians, the name of General José Manuel Hernandez (El Mocho) was put forward as a candidate for the presidency. El Mocho's popularity today seems almost inexplicable, because from a military point of view he had the knack of being constantly defeated. But he was a brave and attractive man, and to the average Venezuelan he appeared as a national champion, the American El Cid. Perhaps the fact that he was of humble birth made him something of a hero with the masses. But when the electoral results for the presidency were published it was Andrade, Crespo's candidate, who headed the lists. Whereupon El Mocho, backed by a large following, rose in revolt, and it was during this revolution that Crespo was killed. Crespo's death was El Mocho's first real break. Politically it gave the Conservative party, the oligarchs, new life, and there was a spate of minor revolutionary uprisings. Thus there is the paradoxical situation of both Hernandez and Andrade being helped by Crespo's death. The entire country was now a seething cauldron, but at that moment in Venezuelan history it was the Andean region which was to play a leading role.

The Andes may be said to be divided into three distinct parts. Alike in many ways, nevertheless they are all very different, and in their differences may be found a key to the problems facing the whole of Venezuela. Trujillo was mainly an agricultural region, but it had suffered a great deal of erosion. During the wars of independence and the innumerable civil wars of the nineteenth century, it had shown an outstanding military spirit. Its caudillos were arrogant, warlike leaders, descendants of the proud Spanish conquistadores, as heroic as they were backward and primitive in their manner and way of thinking. Their tribal, touchy and warlike spirit had made them backward and they still followed the centuries-old agricultural methods practised by their Castilian ancestors. Consequently the region was poor, and both the quality and quantity of the crops was poor. What is important to remember in the power struggle that took place, was that Trujillanos did not believe in a soft and easy life. They did not consider it manly. Their legendary heroes were terrible and stoic. They were the embodiment of a mystic Spain, warlike and knightly in this Venezuela of the nineteenth century, so that they had no qualms in trying to impose their ideas on their fellow countrymen.

Very different from Trujillo was Merida, known perhaps for its academies rather than generals. Politically, Merida relied on its oligarchy, which was at once sceptical and suspicious of the political upheavals which tortured Venezuela after the Federal wars. In her Conservative Congress, Merida boasted many jurists and orators. After the Federal triumph their best men had gone into mourning with Paez's defeat, and they consoled themselves by dedicating their lives to their homes, and the cultivation of their lands. But after Andueza (1890–2), the region of Merida also had to undergo much suffering when the Barlovento General, Antonio Fernandez, came to govern it. Besides the hatred and discontent which Fernandez managed to sow in Merida with his fierce soldiers, the earthquake of April 1894 was another powerful factor for Andean discontent and frustration. During Crespo's term of office, 1892–8, the situation soured and worsened. The Conservative leaders had caused them to suffer many disappointments. Juan Bautista Araujo, a Conservative, had never been very successful with his 'pacts and arrangements' under Guzman. Another leader who failed to fulfil their aspirations was Dr Carlos Rangel Garbiras, descendant of their great local hero Antonio Rangel. In Carlos Rangel they had a possible and able caudillo, a man of arms and letters who might lead them forward to the position they felt was their due in the government of the country. But though

Rangel at one time ruled the State of Los Andes as its President, nevertheless he was not a success and his prestige declined. He was too cultured and aristocratic for the rough Venezuelan democracy at the time, and for the warlike sorties of the 1892–9 era. His personality was eclipsed by a more audacious and vivid figure, namely Cipriano Castro.

Castro came from El Tachira, then the newest of all these lands; also the region that had known less 'historical' action than Trujillo or Merida. Tachira was just beginning to wake up. The process was convulsive, for its people were stubborn, obstinate, perspicacious, far-seeing and hard working. They were different from the romantic warriors of Trujillo, or the oligarchic scholars and dreamers of Merida. Tachira demanded a greater participation in the political life of the country. Their vast coffee plantations had prospered. They were the biggest and best of the entire region. A new impulse and vigour was injected into the area in about 1860 when many people emigrated from Barinas and Merida. The people left their homes in search of land and secure work and the result was that they bestowed an extraordinary vitality and healthy growth to Tachira. Without doubt the Tachirenses had the highest standard of living in the Andes. Tachira was beginning to compete with and produce rivals to the Trujillian caudillos.

On the Liberal side Tachira had its representative in the person of General Espiritu Santo Morales, nicknamed 'El Paton' or 'big-footed'. He could be likened to a Rabelaisian giant. The culture and social prestige which Tachira lacked, and sorely needed, was bestowed by the scholarship of the illustrious Canon José de Jesus, Carrero, Dean of the Cathedral of Merida, and one of the best Latin scholars and canonists of the Andes. All this sense of an awakening to a new life, unfulfilled aspirations, and frustration, meant that Tachira was ready for the emergence of a new leader. Among the younger generation one man, Cipriano Castro, began to be seen as its saviour. Since 1866, Castro had figured in local politics. He was appointed Governor of Tachira by Dr Carlos Rangel Garbiras who was then President of the State of Los Andes, and he ruled Tachira with unusual and commendable prudence, thus achieving a great deal of popular prestige in contrast to the increasing unpopularity of Rangel, who with his aristocratic ways divided his people instead of uniting them. Before his term of office was up, the people were either 'rangelistas' or 'ciprianistas'. From this time may be dated the obstinate rivalry between the two men, which was to be one of the characteristics of the succeeding revolutions. On the surface Rangel had everything in his favour and he should have won. He was much travelled in Europe; he had a wide and influential circle of friends and belonged to the oldest and most powerful families of the cordillera and of Caracas. He was a man of great presence, with a courteous, easy-going manner. Yet the very things which made Castro seem inferior goaded him into an aggressive and obstinate stubbornness, for he had the cockiness and the impertinence of many small men.

As Governor of Tachira, Castro gained both experience of office and of handling men. In 1890 he left the governorship and became Deputy of his province to Congress in Caracas. This gave him the opportunity of meeting the politicians of the day, as well as becoming friendly with Andueza Palacio (President 1890-2). Castro greatly admired Andueza's eloquence and demagogism. He began to plan and intrigue, no longer on a regional scale, but on a larger national one. And though it is important to remember that Castro had a reasonably good education his 'culture' and outlook were narrow minded and provincial, as was his way of thinking. The fact that he hailed from the Andes region made him very conscious of Colombia, and the commercial and border problems which the two sister republics had. But as far as Europe was concerned, Castro knew little or nothing. Inevitably all this was to be reflected later in his dealings with the great European powers. It was during those years that Castro began to lay the foundations for his future political career, and from whatever angle he is viewed Castro is the most original, and for many, among the bravest of the Deputies of 1890. In 1892 he actively defended the 'continuismo' of Andueza. As a result of Crespo's triumph (1892–8) Castro was forced to flee to Colombia where he was exiled for the duration of Crespo's reign. Already he was looked upon as chief and the centre of the Liberal party of the Andes.

The man who forced Castro into exile was the other great Andean leader, General Espiritu Santo Morales. It was to be a constant struggle for power between these two men as the years went by. During his years in exile Castro was accompanied by his best friend Juan Vicente Gomez. The tactics which Castro followed were never to let his image fade in the public mind. From Colombia he never ceased to speak and write in the newspapers until his people felt he was the conscience of the Andinos. In 1893 he took advantage of an amnesty and went to Caracas to try and explain to Crespo the real situation, as he saw it, of Los Andes. But Crespo was too preoccupied with the growing danger of El Mocho and his party, so that he hardly took any notice of Castro whom he later described as too big for his boots. Meanwhile Castro returned to Colombia and there he continued to write.

As the years went by, events in Venezuela were going to develop in Castro's favour. In order to keep effective power Crespo planned who his next candidate would be.[1] Ignacio Andrade was the man he chose, who would do as he was bid and who would keep the presidential seat warm for him. Andrade's attributes were colourless. The very opposite of the romantic Mocho Hernandez. By that time Castro had already convinced himself that he was a suitable presidential candidate. For the Andes the immediate result of these rigged elections was that Antonio Fernandez (the scourge of the Andes) was appointed Minister for War, and 'big footed' Morales, Presi-

---

[1] See the previous chapter. Andrade's election marked the initial structure of the twentieth century with political reality, i.e. the systematic falsification of elections which took place under Gomez: political probity and commercial honesty disappeared.

dent of the State of Los Andes. Both men were Castro's enemies. Thereafter, with Crespo's death, the country was torn by sporadic revolutionary risings. There is the curious phenomenon of Rangel Garbiras invading Venezuela from Colombia. He was doomed to fail since he represented the conservative element, and indeed he was defeated by Morales himself. After this the most advanced element of the Andes, represented by Regulo Olivares and Santiago Briceño Ayesterán, formed a committee of the 'ciprianista' party whilst Castro continued to send propaganda across the border. There was a great deal of general discontent and frustration in the Andes. Castro and Rangel attempted to work together, but this failed. Castro now had everything before him: it was up to him to win or lose everything.

His invasion is essentially 'criollan', and planned on the assumption of the majority of Venezuelan caudillos that war feeds on war, and that it is an inevitable natural phenomenon. Events and life in the Andes were all in Castro's favour. It was a region where rural families were almost tribal, and Castro belonged to them and was therefore backed by them. The country was poor but advancing slowly. Above all it wished to participate in the nation's progress and it deeply resented being frustrated. Those in authority who could have defeated Castro did not believe in Andrade. But they did believe in their future and this future was now in the hands of one of their own.

When Castro governed Tachira he dreamt of ruling all the Andes. Later, when he ruled Venezuela, he dreamed of reviving La Gran Colombia. In his dreams may be found the key to many of the problems arising out of Venezuelan–Colombian relations. The main difficulties which had a direct impact on the policies of the two sister republics were those arising from their frontiers and their commerce. This close link between the Bolivarian countries was one of which the British diplomats were very much aware. Even articles published in the Colombian press attacking foreigners could influence Castro, as well as the party struggles in Colombia itself.

Colombia's troubles with Venezuela regarding her frontier date from 1833. The dissolution of La Gran Colombia had resulted in the dispute of the frontiers between the two nations. In the Neo Granadina Constitution of 1831, Article 2 states that 'the frontiers will be the same ones which in 1810 divided the territories of New Granada from the Captaincy General of Venezuela'. On 11 December 1896 Villiers informed Lord Salisbury that a pamphlet had just been published containing a treaty of peace, friendship and defensive alliance between the republics of Colombia and Venezuela; a treaty of frontier and transient navigation and commerce and on the carrying out of the award of limits between the same republics as well as a Protocol.

The arbitration of the Queen of Spain on the frontier issue between Colombia and Venezuela raised passions and provoked the deepest emotions in Venezuela, but they were particularly sensitive in Tachira and the Andes to anything relating to the Colombian frontiers. Great bitterness was felt concerning the indifference shown by public men in Caracas as well as the press concerning the affairs and economic problems arising out of the Venezuelan–Colombian frontier dispute. Thus this feeling of deep humiliation in the Andes was also one of the prime motives in Castro's rise to power. By 2 March 1898 the situation between Colombia and Venezuela had worsened to such an extent that the Venezuelan representative left Bogota, and Venezuela no longer had a representative in Colombia.

Meanwhile Colombian trade suffered badly from the retaliatory economic measures taken by Venezuela, for Colombia was far more dependent on Venezuela than vice versa.[1] Colombia too was having her difficulties with the United States regarding the Panama Canal project, and as early as 1894

---

[1] Santiago Briceño, (*see* Bibliography). In his letters Santiago Briceño explains in a masterly way the economic difficulties suffered by the Andes region, but difficulties which were less onerous than those undergone by Colombia.

President Caro set great store on the importance of Britain's friendship and support.[1] As far as the United States was concerned a deep resentment prevailed for their interference in South America.[2] Colombia felt that her safety lay with Great Britain and in order to win her friendship she would do her utmost to help her.[3] Thus Colombia was forced to turn to Britain for protection and friendship for she needed her as a bulwark against the ever encroaching power of the United States, and also in her constant struggle against Venezuela.

Castro from the Colombian frontier looked out for his chance, and the dice were weighed in his favour. At that moment he represented a positive hope. He had given many proofs of his energy, independence, personal bravery and warlike qualities. With incredible temerity and fantastic luck he crossed the border, won the first round, and then marched on to the interior of the country. This was to be his first 'folie de grandeur'. The tragedy for Venezuela was that the country believed he was a man: instead they found themselves saddled with a dreamer.

The presidential period of this dreamer is remarkable for only one event of importance, namely the Anglo-German blockade for which Castro must take most of the blame. The international repercussions were perhaps more long lasting than is apparent at first, for it drove the Americans to *define* their policy towards Latin America even though that same

[1] Caro—Resident British Minister, 5 January 1894, F.O. 135/215.

[2] M. Villiers—Salisbury, Treaty No. 1, 7 April 1899, F.O. 135/245. Also Grenvelle and Young, p. 117; 'A good deal of prejudice among a large class of people in Colombia against the United States.'

[3] Villiers—Salisbury, Confidential, Treaty No. 2, 15 April 1899, F.O. 135/245: 'The Minister of Foreign Affairs informed me that he had recently sent instructions to the Colombian Minister in London to aid all in his power the British Government in establishing their territorial claim against Venezuela ... H.E.'s purpose is to cause Great Britain to have rights on the River Orinoco as Venezuela refuses to regard this waterway as international, and has recently levied duties on goods coming to Colombia by that river. The duties are enormous and the trade of Cucúta and other towns has suffered very seriously. The Colombian Government hopes that Great Britain will compel Venezuela to cease this practice.'

policy had long been in their minds. The mistrust and dislike which they enjoy today is part of its legacy. From the domestic point of view the blockade had a traumatic effect on the country, and most particularly on Vicente Gomez, Castro's successor and dictator for twenty-seven years. It confirmed him in his views that the payment of debts was all important if he were to survive. It also established more firmly in his mind the necessity of keeping in with the great powers. This was to affect his policy as regards the petroleum concessions. In brief, Venezuela's humiliation helped to set the course of her unhappy history until well into the twentieth century.

There is no doubt that the international events which took place towards the end of the nineteenth century and the beginning of the twentieth were placing the United Kingdom in the position of handing over the complete hegemony to the United States in the Caribbean. Likewise Venezuela's history since independence days had been the sorry story of her indebtedness, lack of political probity and communal honesty, as well as the ever popular theory that war feeds on war. With this inheritance, and given Castro's character and lack of international knowledge, it is not surprising that he committed all the acts which drove Great Britain and Germany to the use of force. As Bolivar said: 'Proclaim this truth to all men, genius without honesty is but a scourge.'

> 'Di la verdad a los hombres . . . el talento
> sin probidad es un azote.'

Chapter 10

The Blockade

'The world leans to what is true or false or to neither. It shuffles to its purpose, with the crutches it is given. Thus, the world's views fluctuate, like the ebb and flow of the tide.'

'En este mundo traidor
Nada es verdad ni es mentira
Todo es según el color
Del cristal con que se mira.'

Campoamor

When Cipriano Castro seized power in Venezuela, then a country little known and of infinitesimal importance in international politics, events were to converge in such a way that Anglo-American relations would become more defined, and the trends which had been growing over the years, notably that of total American supremacy in the western hemisphere, would henceforth be indisputable.[1]

The Anglo-German blockade of 1902–3, which Castro wished on his unhappy country, likewise helped to bring to a head the idea which for many years had been simmering—'the suspicion in the United States which would seem always to exist if any importance whatever can be attached to an article in the *New York Herald* of the ninth inst. saying that no concert of Powers is wanted or can be tolerated in America. The United States recognises and accepts the responsibility towards European

[1] Dana G. Munro, p. 3.

powers, the responsibility of safeguarding their legitimate commercial interests.' 'It is not quite clear,' the despatch continues, 'whether this article means to convey that the United States on the one hand will not allow any power to assert or enforce its just claims in the South American States, and on the other, accepts full responsibility for policing these states and guaranteeing payment of such claims—in which case they will have their hands full—or whether it is merely warning Germany and Britain not to interfere.[1]

This despatch of Haggard's contains the essence of American policy, a policy which was brought to a head as the blockade crisis developed, for when it ended 'the United States consider that the Monroe Doctrine has been more strongly established and fully recognised.'[2] Before dealing with the events leading directly to the blockade, it is important to note the developments in international history which indirectly focused at this given time. Thus it was that the United Kingdom accepted, even welcomed, America's supremacy in the Caribbean, because of her own world-wide commitments, and also, at this particular time in history, allied herself with such an unpopular bedfellow as Germany was then.

The years 1895–1908 cover a key period in Anglo-German relations. These years also see the end of Salisbury's rule and the taking over of British foreign policy by Landsdowne. It has been said that the Foreign Office saw the world in static terms and applied traditional solutions to new problems. At no time was this more apparent than under Salisbury's aegis, for he tried to maintain 'a masterly inactivity in his foreign policy' and not even the new mood created by the Boer War shocked him out of his general complacency.' Though not particularly optimistic there is no doubt that he worked assiduously for peace according to his beliefs. Salisbury himself described his policy as non-existent for 'we had not got a policy and worked

---

[1] Haggard—Landsdowne, Draft No. III, Confidential, 21 August 1901, F.O. 199/155.

[2] Lascelles—Landsdowne, Berlin, 18 February 1903, F.O. 80/482.

from hand to mouth—with a parliamentary regime like ours it is important not to pledge the Government as to the course it will take in case of some future emergency'.

But in the critical years of the end of the nineteenth century and the beginning of the twentieth century Pax Britanica was fast running out, signalling the end of Salisbury's splendid isolation. Now 'there was a sudden enthusiasm by all the great powers for imperial and naval expansion. Britain was everywhere faced by new rivalries, new pressures which she had never known before.' Landsdowne's character was much more suited than Salisbury's to this situation. His temperament enabled him to tackle the new problems, and the ever-shifting balance of power. To begin with he was more responsive to strategic considerations and he genuinely tried to see the other person's point of view. 'I shouldn't call him clever', Arthur Balfour commented, 'but he was more than competent.'

Thus Landsdowne's tact, his very lack of brilliance or bellicosity aided his efforts to seek a *modus vivendi* with each of the great powers. 'Our conduct has been strictly correct', he wrote to Herbert, and 'the Germans have on the whole behaved well—almost invariably given way to us.' This civilised, dispassionate attitude is apparent in most of his correspondence, even when faced by a great deal of provocation, for he was genuinely alarmed at Britain's isolation, never more apparent than during the Boer War. He was particularly tolerant towards Germany and the Kaiser's extravagances, for the German Emperor, like T. Roosevelt, was obsessed with the superiority of the Anglo-Saxon race.[1] Because Landsdowne had no intention of pursuing an anti-German policy, he was able to bear with these extravagances, as well as the opposition which he encountered in the Foreign Office itself, e.g. from

---

[1] German Emperor to the King, 30 December 1901, F.O. 800/115: 'There is no other race left for God to work His will in and upon except ours; that is I think grounds enough to keep peace and to foster mutual recognition and reciprocity in all that draws us together, and to sink everything which could part us.'

Francis Bertie, to name one.[1] In this policy Landsdowne was fully supported by Sir Frank Lascelles.[2] The two men were in basic agreement and both thought that some kind of arrangement with Germany was possible. It was Lascelles' policy to put the most favourable interpretation on Germany's every action.[3] As for Landsdowne, he was also indifferent to pressure by public opinion and the press, and therefore felt that he could ally himself with Germany over the Venezuelan affair. From Britain's point of view it would have been of little importance, except that it affected the friendly course of Anglo-American relations.[4]

Over and above Landsdowne's search for continental allies was the realisation that it was America's friendship which was of the utmost importance to Great Britain's very existence: 'My business is to think first of all of our relations with the U.S.' The fact that Britain was a great naval and imperial power imposed on her a tremendous strain. Landsdowne saw that Britain had to garner her forces and hand over the defence of the western hemisphere to the United States.

As the first consideration of a rationally conducted foreign policy is to provide for national security, this American friendship was therefore of necessity Landsdowne's chief aim, and when the chips were down during the Anglo-German blockade,

[1] For Bertie's attitude towards Germany and the increasing importance of the United States see Bertie's Memorandum, 1901, F.O. 800/115. Regarding Germany he wrote: 'I do not mention her ambitions in the American seas. They may be safely left to be dealt with by the United States.'

[2] British Ambassador in Berlin from 1895–1905, key period in Anglo-German relations. See G. Monger, p. 21. Landsdowne wrote to Lascelles: 'We should use every effort to maintain, and if we can to strengthen the good relations which at present exist between the Queen's Government and that of the Emperor.'

[3] Lascelles—Landsdowne, Berlin, 18 February 1903, F.O. 80/482.

[4] Herbert—Landsdowne, 4 February 1903, F.O. 800/144: 'Pressure put on me by friends of the administration who state that the President and Mr Hay will be seriously embarrassed and the Alaska Treaty threatened if we do not arrive at an immediate settlement . . . it will impair our good relations with this country.' If only because of this the blockade was of international importance for Great Britain.

he fully accepted her hegemony in the Caribbean. Also, since British interests during these years were more imperilled in Europe, the Mediterranean, and the East, Great Britain pursued a very pro-American policy as regards Cuba, the Philippines, the Isthmian problem and the Alaska boundary question. During the Venezuelan dispute, the fact that the blockade might in any way endanger this relationship encouraged Landsdowne to end the blockade as soon as he possibly could.[1] It was precisely because Castro was so crassly ignorant of international politics that he failed to realise Venezuela's danger, and so precipitated the blockade. Later he also failed to appreciate Great Britain's relationship with the United States, that is to say the importance of America's friendship for the United Kingdom, which would eventually result in the Roosevelt corollary, since Britain herself would be only too glad to hand over the task of 'policeman' to the United States.[2]

If Castro was almost totally ignorant of Great Britain, the latter considered South America a backwater and for any diplomat who was sent out there it meant almost total oblivion. As for Edward VII 'the South American Ministers were beyond the pale and no amount of Foreign Office persuasion could

---

[1] Landsdowne was even willing to sacrifice the Canadians in order to ensure United States friendship: Landsdowne—Herbert, 27 December 1903, F.O. 800/144: 'The President and Mr Hay will be seriously embarrassed and the Alaska Treaty threatened if we did not arrive at an immediate settlement.' Note the date, which was at the height of the blockade crisis. Herbert—Landsdowne, 10 February 1903, F.O. 800/144: 'Some of the opposition to the Alaska Treaty is undoubtedly due to this feeling.' See also Herbert—Landsdowne, 12 February 1903, F.O. 800/144: 'ratification of the Alaska Treaty a pleasant surprise—engineered by the Senate and thanks due to Senator Lodge'. Landsdowne's comment is interesting: 'Ratification has made a good effect here and we are all pleased, you can if you think well say something civil from me to Lodge.'

[2] Herbert himself summed up the importance of America's friendship in a few words: 'As regards our friendly relations with the United States, the settlement with Venezuela has not been arrived at a day too soon', Herbert—Landsdowne, 12 February 1903, F.O. 800/144. Thus if only because the blockade highlighted necessity of America's friendship for Great Britain, the blockade was of international importance.

convince the monarch that their inclusion in a royal party was a boredom worth enduring.' Despite this indifference, economically the continent was still of some importance and besides the renewed interest engendered by the Isthmian question, which also raised strategic considerations,[1] the United Kingdom had more capital invested in Venezuela than the United States or any of her European rivals. Shortly after the blockade, Bax-Ironside, the Resident British Minister in Caracas, wrote to Landsdowne that the interests of the United States in Venezuela from a commercial point of view were minute. Great Britain had invested £12,000,000, Germany £8,000,000, France £6,000,000. The British colony in Caracas was numerically small but nevertheless represented a heavy capital. The German colony was numerically large, and represented a modest capital. The French had small colonies, not only in Caracas but in the majority of the seaboard towns. The Americans had no colony throughout Venezuela, and the amount of money invested was extremely moderate. There were only seven United States citizens in Caracas, whom Bax-Ironside considered men of straw or adventurers. The one exception was the representative of the New York and Bermudez Asphalt Company, which had started to work some asphalt deposits in the interior. But the absolute capital invested by this company in their Venezuelan business amounted to only £100,000. There was no United States railway or large enterprises with the exception of the monopoly enjoyed by the Orinoco Steam Ship Company, and then ships flew until recently the British flag. Therefore the interests of the Americans was little more than academic, and the chief sufferers from the revolutions were undoubtedly the Europeans. This was Bax-Ironside's view. It could be said, however, that the

[1] J. S. Grenville and G. B. Young, p. 267. Also Europeans attached great importance to trade with Latin America and this interest was manifested in the Panama Canal which would be of great strategic and commercial importance. The expansion of trade would counter the effect of the depression at home.

American interest was more political than commercial at this point. It is interesting too that the Venezuelans themselves did not consider the American interest purely academic. Indeed they feared active intervention by them.

The growing German interest also roused fears in Great Britain, not so much from an economic point of view as from a strategic one. As early as 1900 there were well founded rumours that the Imperial Government was attempting to establish a coaling station in the island of Margarita,[1] and when these rumours grew the Colonial Office comment is important in so far as they hoped it would be the Americans who would stop any such action on Germany's part.[2] By 1901 however, Grant Duff was writing from Caracas that a serviceable harbour had been discovered in Margarita, which it was said the German Government would lease for forty years as a coaling station. It was also proposed to exploit the coal mines at Caramichata for the use of the German navy in Caribbean waters. On 9 August 1901, the *New York Herald* declared that no concert of Powers is wanted or can be tolerated in America. As Landsdowne was influenced by strategic considerations, he realised the necessity of handing over the defence of the Caribbean to the Americans, and with the arrival of Fisher at the

[1] Extract from a letter from M. Grant Duff—Mr Larcom. Caracas, 2 December 1900, C.O. 295/400: 'As to Margarita I will try and find out more if possible —I think there is no doubt that the Germans have been trying for a coaling station.' See also Haggard—Landsdowne, 24 September 1900, C.O. 295/400: intention on the part of the Venezuelan Government to make a territorial cession to Germany in settlement of claims of that country (this was the island of Margarita). The presence of German man-of-war *Vineta* had effect of strengthening belief that some kind of territorial cession was contemplated. There was also a German plan for taking over the Eastern region of Venezuela and Guayana—For reference to this see *Boletín del Archivo Histórico de Mira-flores*, No. 9, November–December 1960, p. 4 onwards. César Zumeta's correspondence.

[2] Colonial Office comment 23 October 1900, No. 34586: 'I hope the Americans will have something to say to this.' See following on Germany and Margarita: British Acting Vice Consul W. A. Andral—Landsdowne, No. 39, Caracas, 5 September 1900, C.O. 295/400, Villiers—Colonial Office, 26 September 1900, C.O. No. 31432, C.O. 295/400.

Admiralty in 1904 as First Sea Lord, the reorganisation of the navy would take place, and the North American Squadron's role would disappear. But during the crucial years leading up to and including the Anglo-German blockade, these international politics were influencing the policy of the great powers. The Venezuelan episode appeared to them as of little importance. But for Venezuela herself it was a traumatic experience; it would influence the course of her history during the first three decades of the twentieth century. And as one of the chief exporting oil countries in the world, this humiliation would without doubt have repercussions. This then was the international background at the beginning of the century. It is necessary now to turn to Venezuela's domestic events, in order to realise why Great Britain and Germany were driven to such desperate measures.

When Cipriano Castro overthrew Andrade's Government in October 1899, most of the country welcomed him as a man of action, indeed as a saviour. Perhaps because so much was expected of him, the disillusion was all the greater. In the same way that Landsdowne's character and bent of mind influenced Great Britain's foreign policy, so Cipriano Castro's was to have an impact on his country's history, but unfortunately not to Venezuela's advantage.

Castro's violent, contradictory personality was the product of the crisis which Venezuela herself was undergoing, for it was a quasi heroic, impassionate and libertine age. Cipriano Castro was born on 12 October 1858 in the Andes at San Pedro de Capacho. He was always a small person physically and from an early age saw himself as a Napoleonic figure. This 'Napoleonic conception' of himself must never be forgotten. It is also important to note that Castro's education and trend of mind was purely parochial and that the only contact which he had outside Venezuela was Colombia; of Europe he was woefully ignorant.

Castro's victorious revolutionary campaign is a landmark in Venezuela's history since it heralded the Andino's advent to power which lasted well into the 1930s. Its only importance internationally was that by reaching the presidency Castro precipitated the Anglo-German blockade of 1902–3. That Castro was able to overthrow so successfully Andrade's Government was a symptom of the economic and social crises which the country was undergoing.

This situation was vividly described by Haggard who was informed by an influential Venezuelan that the country was in a state of complete anarchy, and the political outlook was very grave. Both the President (Andrade) and his Government were universally detested and it could be said that the rest of the country would welcome *any* change. Haggard also noted that unless somebody could come forward who was strong enough to repress all these discordant elements, Venezuela had now before her a long period of anarchy. The monetary complications were such that the financial outlook was as bad as the political.

The fact that Cipriano Castro was an Andino undoubtedly played an important part in his seizure of power, for at that time the Andes was the most prosperous and healthy region in the country. Castro's revolution, known as La Restauradora, was a campaign of academics and countryfolk (campesinos); it was likewise a mixture of so-called orators and also of semi-illiterates.

The Andean region had been lucky in managing to escape the three main streams of disasters which had stricken Venezuela. First, the ability of her leaders had steered her people clear of the bloody Federal wars which had devastated the rest of the country. Second, the plague of locusts which had ravaged Venezuela had spared the coffee plantations, the basis of Andean wealth, and also the main source of Venezuela's income. Last but not least the Andes had not succumbed to the malarial fevers which had exhausted the other regions. For these reasons, El Tachira had developed and nursed political aspirations which Caracas ignored. Moreover the Andinos' leading citizens were well educated in Colombian schools.

The proximity and close ties with Colombia were also reflected in Castro's make-up. He was obsessed with Colombia, and this parochial outlook clouded his better judgement. Last but not least, there had been a selective emigration to the Andes from the less prosperous nearby regions, so that the growth of population was well above the national average.

It may be said that taken as a whole Castro's victorious revolution was possible not only because he came from this most vigorous and lively region, backed by people full of frustrated political aspirations, but because Venezuela herself was suffering from a profound economic and social malaise. This in turn engendered political insecurity, fratricidal wars and instability. As Andrade himself said in his defence: 'The various factions in the country never conceded me a day of peace'. Andrade quite rightly blamed his defeat on the abortive military sorties against Castro, and because he was betrayed by his own followers. They had but one thought in mind, to feather their own nest with the new leader.

The other great tragedy which Venezuela could not overcome was the fact that her rulers, at any rate since and including Guzman Blanco, had the fixed idea that Venezuela was their private property. Thus at every turn, instead of tackling the twin evils, the economy and social conditions, the Treasury was robbed for their personal benefit. It was these conditions which made Castro's rise to power possible. It was these same conditions which brought about the blockade, since Venezuela was never in a position, physically and morally, to meet the claims of the great powers.

Castro's presidency was to be dogged by almost continuous revolutions and lack of revenue, so that it was a vicious circle from which Venezuela was unable to extricate herself. In December 1900 Castro's Government managed to resume payments on its debts at the rate of one half of the full amount due each month. The Council of Foreign Bondholders was glad of the partial resumption on account of the service of the external debt. Unfortunately the advice received from the bondholders' agents at Caracas stated that the monthly remittances for the Debt Service were temporarily suspended. This fact would seem to be due to the fresh outbreak of revolutionary movements and the prospects of war with Colombia. In December 1900 Castro notified Boulton (the bondholders' agent) that the Government of Venezuela was prepared to pay, each month, *one half* of the full monthly instalment of Bs.177,933.58 pending the meeting of the Constituent Assembly in February 1901. The bondholders expected in vain that payments *in full* would be resumed and the arrears of interest would be dealt with by the Assembly. The Assembly did not even discuss the matter, and the Government continued to pay *one half* of the regular instalment each month. There was a serious stagnation in trade and the outlook for the rest of the year was not encouraging.

The Report of the Minister of Finance for the year 1901 gives an idea of the difficulties which Castro faced and the measures which he took to mitigate them. According to him he had attempted to place the economy on a sound footing. This undertaking had been most arduous. The Government, on assuming power twenty-six months previously, had found the National Treasury in a state of chaos, the Bank of Venezuela depleted, and a heavy burden of debt weighing upon the nation. The strictest economy had been absolutely necessary. Nevertheless, according to Castro, the administration within its available resources had done all that was possible to revive the national credit, and to meet the serious liabilities incurred by the earlier administrations. In 1901, therefore, the liabilities of the Republic appeared to be in round figures about Bs.245,000,000.

Finally 'approximate interest arrears' for the loans in default for the years 1901–2 stood at £690,910, making the total £26,539,125. From whatever angle, Venezuela's economic position was extremely vulnerable.[1] It is not surprising there-

[1] For Venezuela's further domestic economic difficulties see *Boletín del Archivo Histórico de Miraflores*, Nos. 35 and 36, Caracas, 1965, pp. 105 onwards. Papeles de 1900.

fore, with the added political and economic complications which she had with Trinidad and Colombia, as well as the powerful revolution within the country organised by Matos, that Venezuela was overwhelmed by her difficulties, and failed to meet her foreign liabilities. Whatever happened in Venezuela was of the highest importance to Trinidad, and therefore the commercial and trade relations between the two are of the utmost importance since they also contributed towards the Anglo-German blockade.

The importance of Venezuela to Trinidad is primarily due to her geographical position and her proximity to that country, and the mighty Orinoco river itself. 'There can be no doubt', wrote Haggard 'that this is a matter of the highest importance to Trinidad, for there is no reason why, if the Orinoco were really open to the commerce and trade of Great Britain and of the world, Trinidad should not become an exceedingly prosperous and valuable possession of the Crown.'[1] Moreover, he pointed out that the vast and rich but hitherto practically inaccessible regions on the Orinoco, if opened up to trade, would probably offer a new market to British productions when the civilising influence of commerce, and the wealth and prosperity which it would bring in its train, had 'rendered them less liable to be convulsed by internal revolutions than they now are'. The great bulk of the Orinoco trade was done through Trinidad,[2] which is opposite and only a few miles from the delta.

---

[1] Haggard—Landsdowne, Caracas, 23 September 1902, C.O. 295/415: 'How close and important are the commercial relations between the two countries . . . the commercial interests of the colony are furthermore adversely affected by Venezuelan revolutions in general . . . it is therefore to our advantage that the relations between the colony and Venezuela should be of the most harmonious description.' See excerpt from *Port-of-Spain Gazette*, 12 September 1901, C.O. 295/405.

[2] *Notes on Trade Between Trinidad and the Orinoco*, F.O. 80/458 and sub-enclosure notes on trade between Trinidad and the Orinoco, C.O. 24439, C.O. 295/418. Of the many channels through which the Orinoco reaches the sea, only two are of value for purposes of navigation, the Grand Boca to the extreme south, and the Macareo. 'The interest of Trinidad in the Orinoco is deep because trans-shipment is necessary and this is the only place where it

Unfortunately for Trinidad many obstacles had been persistently and vexatiously put in her way by successive Venezuelan Governments, not least of which was the obnoxious 30 per cent surtax. The Macareo was probably the most important of the mouths of the Orinoco for British trade;[1] it was also of the utmost importance to Colombia for that river, into which the Meta flows, penetrates into the heart of Colombia and is navigable to within a short distance of Bogotá. It was also closed by Venezuela against Colombia, and explains to a large extent Trinidad's and consequently the United Kingdom's support of Colombia. It also explains the tremendous pressure which Colombia exerted in Trinidad whenever she could.[2]

---

can be effected.' See Alfred Moloney, Governor—Colonial Under Secretary of State, Government House, 31 July 1903, F.O. 80/475. See also Collector of Customs, Trinidad—Head of Intelligence, Department of the Board of Trade, 6 May 1902, C.O. 295/413. A serious warning is given of American interest in the Orinoco and its trade, for 'it will be a pity if it is all left to the Americans'.

[1] Haggard—Landsdowne, No. 15, Commercial, Confidential, 23 September 1902, F.O. 420/206. 'Especially that of the Macareo to which Mr McCarthy calls attention. . . . The navigation of the Macareo, which is of great importance as it is the only easily navigable mouth of the Orinoco which falls within the Gulf of Paria. It is through this mouth that most of the trade of the river is carried . . . in smooth water all the way to Trinidad.' See Knollys, Acting-Governor—J. Chamberlain, 15 October 1900, F.O. 199/141.

[2] This same despatch of Haggard's is interesting in that he points out that 'it might be advisable to introduce conditions respecting the question of the navigation of the Orinoco up to the Colombian frontier . . . to settle it once and for all so that this large market might be thrown open . . . and have a far-reaching influence on the future of Trinidad.' See also *Notes on Trade between Trinidad and the Orinoco*, F.O. 80/458 for the importance of the river to Colombia: 'for a very large part of Colombia the Orinoco is the natural outlet . . . Colombia desires such a route'. See also Memorandum by the Collector of Customs, Trinidad, F.O. 80/475 and *Port-of-Spain Gazette*, 24 September 1903, Trade with Venezuela, F.O. 80/475. Also McCarthy—Worthington, Custom House, Trinidad, 6 May 1902, C.O. 295/415. Regarding Colombia and Orinoco: 'The rebellion in progress in Venezuela is likely to be successful and as Colombia has rendered material aid, that Republic will receive as part of the *quid pro quo* the opening of the Orinoco and Zulia.' See McCarthy—Worthington, Trinidad, 6 May 1902, C.O. 295/415. See also Jerningham, Governor of Trinidad—H.M.'s Minister at Bogotá, 24 January 1899, F.O. 135/245.

The obnoxious 30 per cent differential duty was a constant source of friction between Trinidad and Venezuela. It embittered the relations between the two countries, and there is no doubt that it contributed not a little to the blockade crisis.

Besides the fact that Venezuela feared Trinidad and sought to harm her by way of retaliation, there was much opposition to any remission by the great merchant houses in Venezuela, and the President was not prepared to face the opposition which such a step would incur. The President himself feared to offend the three commercial houses of Boulton, Blohar and Lesend by repealing the surcharge. These houses, all of foreign origin, thought that the removal of the surcharge would, by causing Trinidad and perhaps Curacao to become *entre-pôts* for European produce, and by thus lowering the price of imports, reduce their iniquitous profits. As the smaller houses were more or less dependent on them, together they formed a formidable body with which the Venezuelan Government had to reckon. This was particularly so at that date, for the Government had its hands full in the Provinces and was anxious to conciliate the commercial classes in the capital.[1]

It is apparent therefore that Venezuela's relations with Trinidad exacerbated her own economic position, further embittered negotiations with the colony, and also helped to worsen

---

[1] Haggard—Landsdowne, 5 November 1900, C.O. 295/407: It is particularly interesting that the house of Boulton, which called itself English, did more than anybody else to keep the surcharge and thus harmed Trinidad. According to Haggard, Boulton's trade was almost entirely with the States and 'is more or less directly responsible for the first application of this illegal tax by Guzman Blanco. They were mixed up with him in his financial schemes and it is said that it was they who put him up to this means of at once wreaking his spite on Trinidad and putting money into their own pockets . . . they have interested themselves actively since my arrival here, in opposing any redress of the wrong at that time inflicted.' It was particularly ironical that it should be the House of Boulton which was so implicated, since they were the agents for the Council of Foreign Bondholders and subsequently collected the customs dues after the Anglo-German blockade. A further reason for keeping the tax is suggested by Haggard who believed Castro thought 'it gives them a hold over us.' See Haggard—Salisbury, Caracas, 29 July 1899, C.O. No. 22626—C.O. 295/394.

her Colombian policies. It seemed as if all the fates were acting against Venezuela.

It has been said that when Castro came to power, Venezuelans thought they had acquired a man, and they found themselves saddled with a dreamer. In nothing is this more true than in Castro's dealings with Colombia, for he was obsessed with a vision of himself riding at the head of a Venezuelan army, capturing Bogotá, and from thence, who knows, Lima and even Buenos Aires. It has also been said that he once actually intended to march on Bogotá and so informed his Minister of War, General José Ignacio Pulido. The latter tendered his resignation, but not before he had warned Castro to forget his irrational dreams.

In order to understand the situation regarding the two sister republics, it is essential to realise that if Venezuela was torn and wracked by continual revolutions, Colombia herself was in the same disastrous condition. 'Owing to the long duration of the present revolution' wrote Mr Welby the Resident British Minister in Bogotá, 'the state of the country is gradually becoming worse and worse, and the situation will soon be almost intolerable on account of the ruin it is causing to every kind of industry, and the useless and enormous waste of money it has entailed in the purchase of arms . . . nothing could be worse than the present state of affairs in the capital.' In a general review of the situation in 1901, it was likewise stated that this civil war which had broken out in October 1899 had crippled the national industry and paralysed all commercial enterprise with the exterior.

The civil war in Colombia was waged between the two principal parties, namely the Conservatives and Liberals. The Conservative party was in power and was strongly supported by the clergy who feared retaliatory measures on the Church by the Liberals, should they win. The fact that the Liberals were more often than not stronger than the Government itself was probably due to the support which they received from Venezuela. Besides this material help which Castro supplied, he promulgated a decree in October 1900 which was calculated to harm Colombia's trade as much as possible. Welby considered this act on Castro's part as an example of the present state of relations existing between Venezuela and Colombia, for it would greatly harm the 'commerce and interests of this country that it can only be considered on the same ground as their refusal to enter into any agreement at present for the free navigation of the Orinoco'.[1] He had also thought that the Venezuelan Government had been very disappointed over the terms of the late award for the delimitation of the frontier, which were certainly more favourable to Colombia's interests.

Colombia for her part invariably tried to enlist Britain's help against Venezuela when the opportunity presented itself. Dr Martinez Silva, the Minister for Foreign Affairs, requested Welby to forward to Lord Salisbury a translation of the decree issued by the Venezuelan Government, and would appreciate Lord Salisbury's help so that the decree would be rescinded as the shareholders of the Cucutá railway were almost all English. The German Legation's help was also asked, in the interests of the German commercial houses trading at Cucutá.

The Colombian Government likewise was active in promoting a revolution in Venezuela, and as early as July 1900 Castro began to receive news, from the interior of the country and abroad, that Rangel Garbiras was organising a revolution from Colombia with the help of the Colombian Conservative party. The invasion, which lasted only a few days but caused tremendous damage, was reported in the press, and in a vivid, but pronounced anti-Venezuelan bias by Haggard, the Resident British Minister in Caracas. According to Haggard, General Uribe, the Colombian revolutionary leader, was in Maracaibo with 'eight or ten thousand stand of arms and two million cartridges to cross the frontier and renew the revolution'. Haggard also reported that Castro's hostile action had as its object the restoration of Colombia, Venezuela and Ecuador into one state with himself as its head.

[1] Welby—Salisbury, No. 28, 20 October 1900, F.O. 135/251.

Haggard also believed that Colombia had every interest in keeping peace with Venezuela.[1] He did not mention that this was the main reason why she had 'submitted to all sorts of acts of provocation'. When the Venezuelan Government demanded explanations regarding the invasion of Venezuela by Colombian troops, and the Colombian Minister Dr Rico was unable to reply, he was requested to leave. Even then Rico did not break off diplomatic relations. Nevertheless the connections between the two countries were becoming more and more strained, and Colombian consuls in Venezuela had their exequaturs withdrawn, and Venezuelan consuls in Colombia had their letters patent cancelled.

By 15 October 1901 Castro was in an even worse position. Besides his mounting economic difficulties, his troops faced total defeat near Rio Hacha. 'They say it was a complete rout', and a great deal of ammunition was captured by the Colombians. As regards the Anglo-German blockade, what impact if any did these strained relations have? In the first instance, the Colombian Government supported another revolutionary attempt in Venezuela, namely that of Matos known as La Libertadora. Its chief claim to international fame was the notorious incident of the *Ban Righ*, belonging to the Colombian Government, and whose sole object was to raid and harass the coasts of Venezuela.[2] There can be little doubt that the fear

[1] Colombia indeed had everything to lose if she was at war with Venezuela, e.g. the navigation of the Orinoco for one, which was of supreme importance to her. Moreover the United Kingdom had never claimed any right to navigate it, and were not in a position to help Colombia in the matter. See Larcom—Haggard, 28 May 1901, F.O. 199/147.

[2] Haggard—Landsdowne, No. 120, Confidential, 5 September 1901, F.O. 199/156: in the despatch Haggard points out American anxiety regarding the fact that the strained relations between the two South American sister republics might conceivably lead to interference by the great European powers: 'where local South American politics are concerned, which may in any respect, affect directly or indirectly United States interests'. In this despatch Haggard also noted that the German Chargé d'Affaires had requested and obtained for the cruiser *Vineta* to remain in Caribbean waters . . . 'will consequently be at hand in case of necessity'. See also Haggard—Landsdowne, No. 155, Confidential, 29 October 1901, F.O. 199/156, for United States' interest in Venezuelan-

which this ship inspired in the Venezuelan Government was one of the main causes why relations became so strained with the United Kingdom, to the point that the Venezuelan Foreign Ministry refused to deal with the pending claims of the British Government, until the *Ban Righ* affair was resolved. This notorious ship likewise embittered Venezuela's relations even more with Trinidad, since the *Ban Righ* made use of Port of Spain. To this extent Venezuelan–Colombian relations had international repercussions.

Matos' revolution was, as has been said, of little importance internationally except that it worsened considerably Venezuela's relations not only with Colombia but with the United Kingdom, Trinidad and Germany. The revolution made her internal situation, particularly on the economic side, even harder for her to meet her financial liabilities. Before tackling the claims which drove the European powers to such desperate measures, the activities of the notorious *Ban Righ*, once in Caribbean waters and under the command of General Matos, spread terror and dismay. It should be noted that Haggard at this point, unlike his British counterpart in Bogotá, lacked complete sympathy or understanding of Venezuela and her difficulties. In fact it is remarkable how often Haggard defends Colombia against Venezuela, and invariably supported Colombia's point of view.

Venezuela had always feared Trinidad because of her proximity to the Venezuelan coast, which made her a convenient launching place for any potential revolution. There can be little doubt that it was fear, fear of the consequences for Venezuela, which now made the Venezuelan Government so intractable regarding any explanations on the part of Haggard

---

Colombian quarrel. For Colombia's admission that the *Ban Righ* belonged to her, had engaged in various acts of hostility against Venezuela and had put into Port of Spain, acts which gravely embarrassed the British Government, see Spencer S. Dickson—Landsdowne, Bogotá, 14 May 1902, C.O. 295/414. See also Memorandum left with Dr Paul, 2 April 1902. Confidential, F.O. 135/266, stating Britain's difficulties due to *Ban Righ*'s activities.

or the Government of Trinidad regarding the *Ban Righ*. On 14 March 1902 Haggard reported that 'the Venezuelan Government in an exceedingly angry note complains generally of the Trinidad authorities, for allowing the vessel to be reinforced from the colony, of their toleration of the preparation and despatch thence publicly of armed expeditions against Venezuela'.[1]

By the middle of July 1902 the Venezuelan Government was almost beside itself with fear and rage: in two notes to Haggard, Lopez Baralt, the Venezuelan Foreign Minister, protested most solemnly against the *Ban Righ* being recognised by Britain, and moreover considered that the United Kingdom was responsible for acts of piracy since the *Ban Righ* had been despatched from British ports, with the British flag and papers. These piratical acts were directly prejudicial to the commerce, peace and general interests of the Republic.

In the second note which Lopez Baralt sent to Haggard, he was outraged that Haggard had threatened to 'discontinue' the hospitality of British ports to the cruisers of Venezuela, and was horrified at 'the menacing tone' which he believed to be in open

---

[1] For a colourful account of the *Ban Righ* and her activities see *The Venezuelan Herald*, 21 August 1902, F.O. 199/160. Haggard—Landsdowne, No. 20, telegram, 14 March 1902, F.O. 199/162. There is no doubt that Trinidad's relations with Venezuela also influenced the course of events since the Venezuelan Government was so enraged by the colony that they could never see Trinidad's point of view, and vice versa. When pressed, Trinidad admitted that 'there may be some justification for a certain slackness in the repression of smuggling' but said that this was the fault of the 30 per cent surcharge. See Haggard—Landsdowne, 2 November 1901, C.O. 295/407. Because of this deep sense of grievance Trinidad permitted revolutionary activities to be planned from the island. This in turn aroused the Venezuelan Government's fear and rage. See letter in press cutting signed Felix A. Ambard, *The Mirror*, 24 October 1901, C.O. 295/407. For accounts of the ceaseless bickerings between Venezuela and Trinidad see Colonial Office comments—Trinidad, No. 15025, 18 April 1902, C.O. 295/414: 'Mr. Haggard seems to think Trinidad is deliberately encouraging smuggling and the export of arms.' Also C. P. Lucas, Under Secretary of State, Foreign Office, 23 November 1901, F.O. 199/147: 'As regards Venezuela, those in power always look with suspicion and irritation towards this colony as, if not the centre of revolutionary activity, at least a country whence those who are "out" and aim at ousting those who are "in" obtain supplies of rifles and other warlike stores.'

opposition to the two countries' commercial and political relations. Accordingly the Venezuelan Government considered Haggard's expression as inadmissible. At this point Haggard's open antipathy of Venezuela undoubtedly helped to embitter relations between the two countries.[1]

Both the United Kingdom and Venezuela were equally intransigent: that they should have reached this stage was a process of many years as relations between the two became progressively soured. And as the twentieth century unfolded and Venezuela was once more torn apart by revolution and anarchy, all her economic ills multiplied, and her latent fears rose to the surface. In this atmosphere it is not surprising that both countries found it hard, if not impossible, to come to any agreement.[2]

Unfortunately for his country, Castro ignored all the dangers which were becoming more and more apparent every day. Shortly afterwards Haggard was again reporting that the Germans intended to hold Venezuela directly responsible for the just settlement of their claims. Castro's contention was that the Government could not pay because it would mean the country's absolute ruin, a remark which gained him little sympathy from Haggard: 'Whenever these remarks are addressed to me I always reply that it is their own affair, and they cannot expect foreign nations to interest themselves in their private concerns.' At this point Haggard suggested that the Custom Houses should be administered for a prolonged period by one or more foreign powers, since 'the object of

[1] D. C. M. Platt, 'British Diplomacy in Latin America since the Emancipation', reprinted from *Inter-American Affairs*, 21, 3, p. 41: 'The indifferent quality of British Diplomatic Missions in Latin America.'

[2] The Venezuelan Government at this stage was not only threatened by *Ban Righ* but by the extremely fierce fighting taking place in the country, so that she had no respite. In this situation greater and more able statesmen would have found it hard to deal with the pressures that were being exerted on them by the great powers. For some excellent accounts of the revolutionary fighting see volumes A.D.M. 1/7618. See also Haggard—Landsdowne, No. 125, Confidential, 10 September 1901, F.O. 199/156 and enclosed press cutting 'Venezuela and Trinidad', *Port-of-Spain Gazette*, 21 August 1901, F.O. 199/156.

every revolution here is to get possession of the revenue which is chiefly furnished by the Custom Houses . . . this revenue to be devoted to the private necessities of the political administrator and his supporters.' According to Haggard, the revenue would then be diverted to its legitimate channels and the prize of government would no longer be worth fighting for, revolutions would cease and prosperity and wealth would follow. This idea also foreshadows Roosevelt's later policy towards the Latin American republics. By the end of October, the American Minister in Caracas had said that in his view any action of the United States in interfering with Germany in securing her just claims would be simply to assist and encourage robbery. Thus slowly but surely the 'Venezuelan affair' was driving the United States to clarify and proclaim her future policy towards the American republics.

There was, however, a certain jealousy in Washington of German action in Venezuela for 'Germany had, to say the least, an eye on the south of Brazil'.[1] Whatever Germany's aspirations, however, she was not prepared to risk the displeasure of the United States for before any intervention took place in Venezuela 'it would be necessary to obtain the concurrence of the United States Government'. Once again this underlies the importance of the Venezuelan incident, since Germany at this stage acknowledged the supremacy of the United States in the Caribbean. By December of that year the German Ambassador in Washington had told the President that any proposed action against Venezuela would be entirely confined to the enforcement of her claims, and had no ulterior motive of territorial aggrandisement. Germany therefore was not likely to run any serious risk of incurring the active animosity of the United States for the sake of a foothold in Venezuela. From the American point of view it meant that the Monroe Doctrine

---

[1] See press cutting entitled *South America, The Country on Which the Kaiser has his Eye*, F.O. 80/80/458: 'Countries at once so rich and so unstable offer a tempting bait to European powers, and there is little doubt that the astute Kaiser has his eye on South America.'

was fully accepted by the European powers. This was further
endorsed by a published telegram sent to Caracas from Washington to the effect that the German Government had come to
an agreement with the United States, by which, on condition
that there would be no taking possession of any territory,
Germany or any other power may 'enforce the payment of its
claims in Venezuela and may even send a fleet for that purpose'.
Although President Roosevelt was determined to uphold the
principles of the Monroe Doctrine, he did not intend to stand
in the way of the powers enforcing their lawful claims, nor did
he intend to screen any South American republic who had to
give lawful satisfaction for these. Gradually but none the less
surely, American policy was being made clear, the policy that
was to play such an important role in the first quarter of the
century.

Yet despite these many warnings, Castro took no heed.
According to Haggard he had assumed his usual defiant attitude
stating that if 'the Germans advanced upon Caracas—he
proposed to destroy them as the Boers destroyed the British,
so if the Germans do not act now, after so much parade, he will
believe that it was because they were afraid of his threats and
he will act on that belief.'

The attitude of the British Government remained one of
caution. As far as the United Kingdom was concerned, they
were willing to co-operate with Germany but only 'if the
United States do not object to such action'. There was also a
pronounced bias against Germany, an attitude not shared by
Landsdowne. In the same document the Colonial Office commented: 'Personally, I am inclined to be sceptical about
Germany's supposed intentions', and the warning that 'I should
leave Germany to pull the chestnuts out of the fire. Joint action
with any European power, anywhere, has not been brilliantly
successful in the past . . . and would not be popular, with
Germany, at this moment'. The Colonial Office reflected the
influence of public opinion far more accurately than did Landsdowne.

During the early months of 1902, the *Ban Righ* incident and the growing pressure for British claims to be met contributed, as has been seen, to the impasse between the two countries. Obviously the United Kingdom, once it realised that the Germans meant business, claimed the same treatment as that which was to be accorded to German subjects. And as relations became more strained, outrages were perpetrated against British subjects and property, which only helped to worsen the situation. Since it was the German Government, however, which made the first decisive moves, regarding coercive or threatening measures against Venezuela, it is important to note that Venezuela did not deny the claims, but did reserve the right to decide the justice of these claims. 'The Imperial Government wishes to consider by herself, and to decide herself alone, on the character, amount and manner of payment of claims concerning estates and interests fixed in the Republic, and the Venezuelan Government, relying on the constitution and on the ordinances regulating its working, maintain that suchlike proceedings can be attributed only to their respective national authorities . . . to set this aside would be to deny to the nation the efficacy of its own laws for the due protection of common interests.'[1]

Today, quite rightly, there is little sympathy in Venezuela for Castro or his policies. But the fact remains that Venezuela considered it justifiable to assert her national sovereignty within her own territory: 'To legislate only for nationals and to leave open to foreigners the enjoyment of a special jurisprudence exercised through the intervention of the representatives of other governments, would be to expose countries which are destined to grow through immigration, to degenerate into simple trading houses to the injury of that proper quality of political states which they hold in the international concert.'[2]

[1] The Venezuelan Memorandum to friendly powers concerning German claims—R. Lopez Baralt, Caracas, 12 August 1902, F.O. 199/165.

[2] *The Venezuelan Memorandum to Friendly Powers Concerning German Claims*, F.O. 199/165. Thus in the latter part of the century Venezuela's view has come

This view of Venezuela's is now accepted by the majority of nations: this assertion of Venezuela's is therefore of some importance despite the fact that 'the claims of 1902–3 were legitimate in international law'.[1]

As the increasingly acrimonious correspondence between Venezuela, Great Britain and Germany grew, so the domestic situation in Venezuela itself deteriorated. The rupture came on 7 December when Haggard issued his ultimatum. Since Venezuela did not wish to meet the claims which had arisen in consequence of the late civil war, and previous civil wars, the maltreatment or false imprisonment of British subjects, as well as a settlement of the external debt, Germany and Britain had agreed to act together in order to obtain a settlement of all their claims.

The note ended with the ominous words: 'I am further instructed by H.M.'s Government to make it clear that this communication must be regarded in the light of an ultimatum'. After this, the events took their inexorable course. For the two great powers Britain and Germany, the whole affair was of little importance except in so far as it affected their relations with the United States. At one time it seemed as if the whole blockade had hardly been worthwhile, for the claims were small in pecuniary amount. In the words of Herbert, Britain's ambassador in Washington, 'The time had come for Great Britain to choose between Germany and the United States'. As Herbert saw it, the main benefit for the United Kingdom would probably be that the anti-German feeling which had been roused in the United States could not fail to be of benefit in the long run to Anglo-German relations . . . 'Germany is now

---

to be accepted by the great powers. See press article *South Wales Daily News*, 10 February 1903, article 'Anglo–German Coalition': 'The principle of international right that foreigners are subject to the jurisdiction of the laws and authorities of the country where they reside.'

[1] D. C. M. Platt, 'The Allied Coercion of Venezuela 1902–3, A Reassessment', *Inter-American Economic Affairs*, 15, 4, Spring 1962, p. 27. For a refutation of this viewpoint see Simon Planas-Suarez (*see* Bibliography).

taking place in the American mind as the "natural foe" and the more general feeling becomes, the more the American people will be instinctively drawn towards the people of Great Britain'. It was obvious, however, that this theory would not hold good if Great Britain was in any way associated with Germany in the future. To that extent the blockade had a pronounced effect on Anglo-American relations.

As regards Germany, she too was equally relieved at the conclusion. 'A tone of relief pervades the German press since the news of the settlement of the Venezuelan question reached Berlin.' One or two points may be noticed in this despatch. For Germany, the blockade proved that she could now be regarded as having assumed her place among naval powers. She also considered that her claims had been practically made good. They did not consider the risk of further entanglements would have been worth their while, and they also acknowledged that the United States had considered the Monroe Doctrine had been more strongly established and fully recognised.

In practical terms, the protocols signed by the blockading powers and Venezuela at Washington, 13 February 1903, related to the settlement of their claims and other matters. Certain questions were to be referred to the permanent court of arbitration at The Hague, and for a decision on the claims by a mixed commission. The point of the Hague tribunal was whether the blockading powers should have preference over non-blockading claimants' powers. It was decided in favour of Great Britain and Germany. In the words of W. L. Penfield, Solicitor of the State Department, by asserting the rights of intervention, it foreshadowed the triumph of force in the American continent.[1] The pattern of American policy in the Caribbean was now set for the first decades of the twentieth century: 'Now that the Monroe Doctrine has, through their action in Venezuela, received the virtual sanction of both

[1] Article entitled 'The Anglo–German Intervention in Venezuela' by W. L. Penfield, enclosed in despatch from British Embassy—Landsdowne, 8 July 1903, F.O. 60/486.

Great Britain and Germany, and the implicit approval of the other powers, it becomes only a question of time that the United States should gradually assume charge of the South American republics. In those circumstances it is interesting to enquire how the smaller states will like the process, and how they are for the present disposed towards the nation whom destiny seems to have designated as their future masters. . . . The feeling of South Americans towards their Northern brethren . . . is largely one of suspicion, not unmingled with fear'.[1] The Anglo-German blockade and the ensuing results did not a little to contribute towards these feelings.

[1] Press cutting entitled 'The Two Americas, South's Feeling Towards the North', F.O. 80/458.

Chapter 11

❦

The Summing Up

'Let the pressure of increasing difficulties bring about the inevitable result. Without our intervention they cannot pay, and unless they pay they cannot stay in power.' Dana G. Munro (*see* Bibliography).

These few words embody the reason for the intervention policy. There appear to be two schools of thought regarding the importance of the Venezuelan blockade. It has been said that seen in its correct context, and with proper regard for detail, there was nothing in the Venezuelan affair which could possibly have justified the polemic resulting from it. Also that it can hardly be maintained, in the light of evidence provided by the Foreign Office papers, that this was a bondholders' war, or indeed that it involved any notable departure from the normal and accepted principles of international law.[1]

But the importance of the blockade does not depend on whether or not it was a bondholders' war, or that it involved any notable departure from the normal and accepted principles of international law.[2] Venezuela's incapability of paying her debts, rightly or wrongly, was certainly not unique.[3] What was peculiar to the Anglo-German blockade was that at that time no other country was made to suffer the humiliations Venezuela had to undergo.

[1] D. C. M. Platt, 'The Allied Coercion of Venezuela 1902–3: A Reassessment', *International Economic Affairs*, **15**, 4, Spring 1962, pp. 27–8.

[2] For the Venezuelan viewpoint regarding these two matters see Simon Planas-Suarez; Edgardo Vivas-Salas; J. L. Salcedo-Bastardo.

[3] Planas-Suarez, *op. cit.*, p. 341.

With hindsight it is easy to over-simplify, but the importance of the Anglo-German blockade lies in that it was not until
after it took place that the Roosevelt corollary became an
integral part of the American Government's policy in the
Caribbean. The blockade was without doubt a great help in
clarifying Roosevelt's ideas. He was determined that the
United States should be recognised as a great power, and that
it should behave as a great power, according to his lights. One
of the reasons why he was unable to impose this idea on Great
Britain and alter the balance on Anglo-American relations as
regards the Caribbean was partly due to the thirty-odd years
between 1880 and the outbreak of the First World War which
saw the fulfilment of the economist's prophecy in 1851, the
superiority of the United States over Britain. It was America
triumphant. Britain had led the way in the age of steam,
whereas the United States led in the age of electricity, and
America's 'Manifest Destiny' was truculently proclaimed by
the President of the American Bankers' Association, in a speech
in Denver in 1898, the year of the Spanish American war.
According to the banker, America held the three winning cards
in the game for commercial greatness: iron, steel and coal.
The United States had long been the granary of the world, but
now aspired to be its workshop, and then its clearing house.[1]
To make matters worse for Britain, its position in the Caribbean,
to which admittedly it attached no excessive importance, was
increasingly threatened by the United States, for Roosevelt
had no illusions and was willing to take advantage of every
situation. 'On the whole', he remarked to Lodge in 1901, 'I am
friendly to Britain . . . but I do not at all believe in being over-
effusive or forgetting that fundamentally we are two different
nations.'[2] He had now reached the point when he envisaged a
Caribbean Sea with all European influence eliminated, and
this is of far greater importance than that he probably drama-
tised and heightened the part he played in the blockade affair.

[1] Eric Williams, pp. 120–3.
[2] Henry F. Pringle, p. 280.

Venezuela, the key to the Caribbean, for the second time in a few years had unwittingly driven the United States to assert its hegemony in the western hemisphere. In 1896, Roosevelt had praised the manner in which President Cleveland had been handling the dispute with Great Britain on the Venezuelan boundary. Primarily, he wrote that American action was based on national self-interest. In other words it was patriotic.[1] Now, apart from the fact of getting Britain and Germany to recognise the Monroe Doctrine as regards the Venezuelan affair,[2] the Anglo-German blockade was also the first occasion when European powers had notified the United States before taking action against a Latin American government.[3]

According to an article by W. L. Penfield,[4] the Anglo-German blockade must be considered of international importance because of the repercussions which resulted: 'measured by its consequence, the intervention of Germany and Great Britain in Venezuela was a notable event in its relation to the law of nations. It was notable . . . as an impressive assertion of the right of intervention for the protection of subjects of intervening states . . . and not less important and far-reaching are the consequences which will flow from the recognition of the Monroe Doctrine, and from the reference to the Hague Tribunal.'

Thus the Venezuelan blockade forced on the United States the realisation that any European military action against an

[1] Pringle, p. 279. Actually it was Santo Domingo, otherwise quite unimportant in history, that brought forth the Roosevelt corollary. But already in 1901 Gil Fortoul was writing from Liverpool that most of the press emphasised that the U.S. was determined to show her predominance in all matters relating to South America. *Boletín del Archivo Histórico de Miraflores*, Nos. 35 and 36, Caracas, 1965, p. 71.

[2] *Report of the Council of the Corporation of Bondholders*, London, 1912.

[3] Letter to Grover Cleveland, 26 December 1902, *Letters*, III, p. 398.

[4] Solicitor to the State Department, the article appeared in the July number of the *North American Review* entitled 'The Anglo–German Intervention in Venezuela' enclosed in despatch from British Embassy, Newport, R.I. to Landsdowne, 8 July 1903, F.O. 60/486.

American state could cause an embarrassment and that therefore similar episodes must be prevented in future. The Hague Court's decision made it more, rather than less, probable that similar events should occur. It put a premium on violence.[1]

The Venezuelan affair also marked Roosevelt's first amplification of the Monroe Doctrine: that the mere threat of territorial aggrandisement by a European power was sufficient to justify intervention.[2] Next came the theory that smaller nations must not misbehave and thereby annoy Europe:[3] 'if we are willing to let Germany or Britain act as the policeman of the Caribbean, then we can afford not to interfere when gross wrong-doing occurs. But if we intend to say "hands off" to the powers of Europe, sooner or later we must keep order ourselves.'[4] Admittedly at that period it would have seemed basically wrong to insist that other governments should not use force to compel respect for what they considered their rights: but intervention could be averted if the Caribbean states could attain stable governments and could pay their debts. It was this idea, made explicit in the Roosevelt corollary, that shaped the policy of the United States in the Caribbean roughly during the first quarter of the twentieth century. Therefore, from an international point of view the Venezuelan affair seems fully to justify Penfield's opinion that, measured by its consequences, it was a notable event in its relation to the law of nations.

As regards Latin America the blockade's importance may be found in the words 'stability and payment of debts', the lack of which augmented the U.S.'s intervention policy. It was a policy which sends a shudder of horror throughout Latin America today, and is to some extent still responsible for much anti-American feeling in the American continent.

---

[1] Munro, pp. 75–6.

[2] British Embassy, Newport, R.I.—Landsdowne, 8 July 1903, F.O. 60/486. This was fully acknowledged by H.M.'s Government. On 16 December 1902, Lord Cranbourne announced in the House of Commons that Britain was anxious to assist the United States in maintaining the Monroe Doctrine.

[3] Pringle, pp. 293–5.

[4] Pringle, *Works*, **XV**, p. 257.

In 1908 the astute Juan Vicente Gomez overthrew Castro and seized power. It seemed as if the whole farce would be repeated yet once again, and that Venezuela would go through the sham movements of a change of government. This pattern, however, was now to be altered. The lesson of the Anglo-German blockade had sunk deep into the cunning mind of this bloodthirsty tyrant who was to rule Venezuela for twenty-seven years. He knew that to survive he must achieve two objects: stability and payment of debts. Stability he could attain by crushing all opposition ruthlessly. But unlike his predecessors Gomez would make his rule doubly secure by winning over the great powers. He knew that to survive for any length of time he must avoid Castro's mistake of non-payment of debts, and even in this, history was on Gomez's side. Venezuela's petroleum industry was just beginning, and Gomez now set out to achieve the lesson the Anglo-German blockade had taught him: he would wipe out Venezuela's debts. By 1930 'Venezuela has paid off the full outstanding principal and the current coupon upon her external debt'.[1] In 1929 Gomez was able to announce that the budget expenditure had been fully met although it was four times larger than that of 1909. Venezuela could look forward to the future with confidence.[2] It was, however, a future shaped by Gomez, with all its resultant evils.

Venezuela's privileged geographical position has made her the key to the Caribbean. In the modern world she is of some account. The foregoing chapters have shown her a country gifted beyond compare, 'inhabited by people where the principles of democracy have struck deeper roots than in any other part of Spanish America'[3] but a country nevertheless which was characterised for years by anarchy, revolution and

---

[1] *57th Annual Report of Corporation of Council of Foreign Bondholders*, 1930.

[2] *56th Annual Report of Corporation of Foreign Bondholders*, 1929, p. 409. For a vivid account of how Gomez 'sold' his country see Romulo Betancourt, Part I.

[3] Wilson—Aberdeen, 7 August 1864, No. 45, F.O. 80/390.

autocracy. If it were not so tragic, Venezuela's years of despotic caudillism, disfiguring her from 1870–1935, might be likened to comic opera, where the chief protagonists rose to power through brute force, deluding their followers with vain promises of equality and social justice.

As shown, Guzman Blanco, with his undoubted financial ability, successfully garnered his immense fortune at the expense of the unhappy British bondholders. He also multiplied the already heavy financial burdens of his country, without ever tackling the root of Venezuela's ills, her economy and social conditions.

Castro was a weak imitation, and when it came to the crunch the great powers, Britain and Germany, called his bluff and exposed him for what he was. The Anglo-German blockade left its mark on Venezuela's history; but over and above this it affected the attitude of Latin Americans towards the United States. 'It may be said that U.S. relations with Latin America have been so close, and the interaction of the two parties so constant, that even the internal problems of the Latin American countries have become international problems. This holds as much for the Latin Americans, who cannot attempt to solve their problems without taking into account their position *vis-à-vis* the United States, as for the North Americans, who cannot avoid taking into consideration the effects on their own national interest of the solutions the Latin Americans find for their problems.'[1]

The history of Venezuela, leading up to the Anglo-German blockade, is an attempt to try and understand the growing pains of a small nation, jealous of her national sovereignty as regards her relations with the great powers. Today this seems particularly relevant, when so many small nations' rights are at stake. Otherwise 'what good came of it?' as little Peterkin asked of the Battle of Blenheim.

[1] Victor Alba, pp. 245–63.

Bibliography

Primary Sources

Public Record Office, Chancery Lane: the Venezuelan vols F.O. 200/, F.O. 80/, F.O. 199/, for the relevant years. Trinidad C.O. 295/, Colombia F.O. 135/, A.D.M. 1/7772. Landsdowne papers: F.O. 800/113, 114, 115, 116.

British Museum, Colindale, for the press of the period.

Historical Research Department, British Railways, for railway concessions granted by Guzman Blanco.

Joseph Chamberlain Library, Birmingham.

Council of Foreign Bondholders.

The Old India Office Library, Lord Curzon and Lord George Hamilton Papers.

From Venezuela

The Papers of Relaciones Exteriores, the relevant years, diplomatic and consular.

Palacio de Miraflores, mainly files of Cipriano Castro.

Extensive use of the *Boletín Histórico de Miraflores*.

Some use of family papers from my great uncle Manuel Fombona, who was at the head of the permanent staff of the Venezuelan Foreign Office at the time of the Anglo–German blockade, and some years previous to this.

Acosta, Cecilio, Works, Vol. 9, Caracas, 1961.

Alamo Ybarra, Carlos. *Nuestras Fronteras Occidentales*, Caracas, 1927.

Alba, Victor. *The Latin Americans*, New York, 1969.

Allen, H. C. *The Anglo-American Relationship since 1783*, London, 1939.

Allen, H. C. *Great Britain and the United States, 1753–1952*, London, 1954.

Arcaya, Pedro Manuel. *Historia de las Reclamaciones contra Venezuela*, Caracas, 1964.

Archivo del Mariscal Falcon, Tomo V, Caracas, 1959.

Arellano Moreno, A. *Origenes de la economía Venezolana*, Mejico, 1947.

Autobiography of Andrew D. White, Vols. I and II, London, 1905.

Bacon, R. H. *The Life of Lord Fisher of Kilverstone*, Vols. I and II, London, 1929.

Bailey, Thomas A. *A Diplomatic History of the American People*, 6th edition, New York, 1958.

Bailey and Nasatier. *Latin America*, London, 1960.

Barry, William. *Venezuela*, 1st edition, London, 1886.

Betancourt, Romulo. *Venezuela, Politica y Petroleo*, Puerto Rico, 1955.

Bishop, Jordan. *Latin America and Revolution*, London, 1965.

Blanco-Fombona, Rufino. *La Evolución de las ideas en Venezuela durante la revolución de independencia*, Boletín de la A. N. de la Historia, No. 80.

Blanco-Fombona, Rufino. *El conquistador español del siglo XVI* and *Mocedades de Bolivar*, Caracas, 1943.

Bourne, Kenneth. *The Foreign Policy of Victorian England*, Oxford, 1970.

Brandt, Carlos. *Bajo la tiranía de Cipriano Castro*, Caracas, 1952.

Briceño Iragorry, Mario. *Ideario Politico*, Caracas, 1958.

Briceño, Santiago. *Cartas sobre El Tachiro*, Caracas, 1961.

Briceño, Santiago. *Memorias de su Vida, Militar y Politica*, Caracas, 1948.

Bruce, Maurice. *The Shaping of the Modern World 1870–1939*, London, 1958.

Calvert, Peter. *The Mexican Revolution, 1910–1914*, Cambridge, 1968.

Calvo, Charles. *Le Droit International*, Vol. I, 2nd ed., Paris, 1870.

Campbell, A. E. *Great Britain and the United States, 1895–1903*, London, 1960.

Carr, R. *Latin America Affairs*, Oxford, 1970.

Castellanos, R. R. *Guzman Blanco*, Caracas, 1969.

Cavalier German. *La Política Internacional de Colombia*, Tomo II, 1860–1903, Bogota, 1959.

Corbett, Julian. *Some Principles of Maritime Strategy*, London, 1911.

Daris Maldonado, Samuel. *Tierra Nuestra*, Caracas, 1961.

Diaz-Sanchez, Ramon. *Elipse de una ambición de poder*, Caracas, 1953, 3rd edition.

Dexter-Perkins. *A History of the Monroe Doctrine*, London, 1960.

Documentos para la historia de Guzman Blanco, Caracas, 1876.

Eastwick, Edward B. *Venezuela o apuntes de una republica Sud-Americana en la Historia del Emprestito de 1864*, Caracas, 1959.

Bibliography

Eder, P. J. *Colombia*, London, 1913.

Fisher, John. *Records*, London, 1919.

Fonseca, A. *Origenes Trujillanos*, Caracas, 1955.

Gil Fortoul, José. *Obras Completas*, Vol. IV *Filosofía Constitucional*, Caracas, 1956.

Gil Fortoul, José. *Historia Constitucional de Venezuela*, Tomo III, 4th edition, Caracas, 1954.

Gil Fortoul, José. *Historia Constitucional de Venezuela*, Tomo II, Berlin, 1909.

Gil Fortoul, José. *Historia Constitucional de Venezuela*, Tomo I, Berlin, 1907.

Gilmore, Robert L. *Caudillism and Militarism in Venezuela*, Ohio, 1964.

Gimenez-Rodriguez, G. E. *Versión General del Bloqueo a Venezuela 1902–1903*, article in Review 'Fuerzas Armadas de Venezuela' enero 1960, No. 163.

Gomez, R. A. *Government and Politics in Latin America*, New York, 1965.

Gonzalez Guinan, F. *Historia del Gobierno de la Aclamación 1886–1887*, Caracas, 1899.

Gonzalez Guinan, F. *Historia Contemporánea de Venezuela*, Tomo XIV, Caracas, 1954, y Tomo undecimo 1924—Tomo Decimo cuarto, Caracas, 1925.

Gonzalez, Juan Vicente. *La Doctrina Conservadora*, Vol. II, Caracas.

Grenville, J. S., and Young, G. B. *Politics—Strategy and American Diplomacy*, London, 1960.

Grenville, J. A. S. *Lord Salisbury and Foreign Policy at the Close of the 19th Century*, London, 1964.

Henao y Arrubla. *Historia de Colombia*, Bogotá, 1967.

Herring, Hubert. *A History of Latin America*, New York, 1961.

Hofstadter, Richard. *The American Political Tradition*, London, 1962.

Humphreys, R. A. *Tradition and Revolt in Latin America*, London, 1969.

Izard, Miguel. *La Venezuela del café vista por los viajeros del siglo XIX*, Caracas, 1969.

Jarman, T. L. *Democracy and World Conflict*, London, 1963.

Johnson, John F. *The Military and Society in Latin America*, Stanford, California, 1968.

Lameda y Laudaeta. *Historia Militar y Politica del General J. Crespo*, Vols. I and II, Caracas, 1897.

Lander, Tomas. *La Doctrina Liberal*, Caracas, 1961.

Langer, William L. *European Alliances and Alignments 1871–1890*, New York, 1964.

Langer, William, L. *The Diplomacy of Imperialism*, New York, 1950.

Lemmo, Angelina. *La Educación en Venezuela en 1870*, Caracas, 1961.

Leuchtenburg, William E. *The New Nationalism—Theodore Roosevelt*, New York, 1961.

Lieuwen, E. *United States Policy in South America*, London, 1965.

Lieuwen, E. *Venezuela*, 2nd edition, London, 1965.

Lieuwen, E. *Aims and Politics in Latin America*, New York, 1961.

Link, Arthur S. *Woodrow Wilson and the Progressive Era*, New York, 1954.

Lippmann, Walter. *United States Foreign Policy*, Boston, 1943.

Lopez-Contueras, E. *Páginas para la historia militar de Venezuela*, Caracas, 1945.

Lopez Mendez, Luis. *Obras completas*, Caracas, 1901.

Mahan, Captain A. T. *The Life of Nelson, the Embodiment of the Sea Power of Great Britain*, London, 1899.

Mahan, Captain A. T. *The Influence of Sea Power upon History 1660–1783*, London, 1889.

Manning, W. R. (ed.) *Diplomatic Correspondence of the United States concerning the Independence of the Latin American Nations*, 3 vols. New York, 1925.

Matos, M. A. *Recuerdos*, Caracas, 1927.

Matthews, Herbert. (ed.) *The United States and Latin America*, New York, 1963.

Merk, Frederick. *Manifest and Mission in American History*, New York, 1963.

Middleton. *Records and Reactions, 1856–1939*, London, 1939.

Monger, George. *The End of Isolation*, London, 1963. British Foreign Policy 1900–1907.

Moran, Lieutenant Colonel Manuel. *Las Multitudes y la tropa—Fragmentos*

Bibliography

del curso de educacion moral. Revista del Ejercito Marino y Aeronautica, XXIII, agosto, 1937.

Munro, Dana Gardner. *Intervention and Dollar Diplomacy in the Caribbean 1900–1921*, New Jersey, 1964.

Munro, Dana Gardner. *The Latin American Republics*, London, 3rd edition, 1961.

Navarra, N. E. *Eclesiasticos Venezolanos*, Caracas, 1951.

Neale, R. G. *Britain and American Imperialism 1898–1900*, Brisbane, 1965.

Nevins, A. *Henry White, Thirty Years of American Diplomacy*, London, 1930.

Oropesa, Juan. *Cuatro siglos de Historia Venezolana*, Caracas, 1947.

Paredes, Antonio. *Como Ilegó Cipriano Castro al poder*, Caracas, 1954.

Pendle, George. *A History of Latin America*, London, 1967.

Perkins, Bradford. *The Great Rapprochement—England and the United States, 1895–1914*, London, 1969.

Petre, F. Loraine. *The Republic of Colombia*, 1906.

Picon-Salas, Mariano. *Comprension de Venezuela*, Caracas, 1949.

Picon-Salas, Mariano. *Los días de Cipriano Castro*, Caracas, 1953.

Pike, Frederick B. *Freedom and Reform in Latin America*, Notre Dame, 1967.

Planas-Suarez, Simon. *El conflicto Venezolano*, Buenos Aires, 1963.

Platt, D. C. M. *British Bondholders in the 19th Century Latin America, Injury and Remedy*.

Platt, D. C. M. *Finance, Trade and Politics in British Foreign 1815–1914*, Oxford, 1968.

Ponte, Andres F. *Bolivar y otros ensayos*, Caracas, 1919.

Pringle, Henry F. *Theodore Roosevelt*, London, 1932.

Pullido Mendez, Manuel A. *Regulo Olivares y su epoca*, Caracas, 1961.

Rojas, Pedro José. *La Doctrina Conservadora*, Tomo II, Caracas, 1961.

Rippy, J. F. *British Investments in Latin America 1822–1949*, Minneapolis, 1959.

Rippy, J. F. *Latin America—A Modern History*, Michigan, 1959.

Salcedo-Bastardo, J. L. *Historia Fundamental de Venezuela*, Caracas.

Schneider and Kingsbury. *An Atlas of Latin American Affairs*, London, 1966.

Schuman. *The Education of a Navy—The Development of British Naval Strategic Thought 1867–1914*, London, 1965.

Siso Martinez, J. M. *Historia de Venezuela*, Caracas, 1970.

Statesmen's Year Book, 1887.

Steiner, Zara. *The Foreign Office and Foreign Policy, 1898–1914*, Cambridge, 1969.

Tavlia Acosta, B. *Rio Negro*, Maracay, 1927.

Thurber, O. E. *Origen del capital Norteamericana en Venezuela*, translated Angel Raul Villasana Barquisimeto, 1955.

Toro Elias. *Fermin Toro*, Caracas, 1952.

Tosta Virgilio. *El Caudillismo según once autores Venezolanos*, Caracas, 1945.

Usher, Roland. *Pan-Americanism*, London, 1915.

Vila, Marco Aurelio. *Geografía del Tachira*, Caracas, 1957.

Vila, Marco Aurelio. *Aspectos Geográficos del Estado*, Miranda—Caracas, 1967.

Villafañe, José Gregorio. *Apuntes estadisticos del Tachira*, Caracas, 1901.

Vallenilla Lanz, Laureano. *Cesarismo democrático*, Caracas, 1961.

Vallenilla Lanz, Laureano. *Escrito de Memoria*, Versailles, 1961.

Vivas-Salas, Edgardo. *Nueva interpretación de la crisis internacional Venezolana de 1902–3*, segunda edición, San Cristóbal, no date.

Whitaker, Arthur P. *The United States of South America—The Northern Republics*, London, 1948.

Wilbur and Halsey. *The Monroe Doctrine*, London, 1965.

Wilgus, A. C., and d'Eca, R. *Latin American History*, New York, 1963 edition.

Williams, Eric. *British Historians and the West Indies*, Port of Spain, 1964.

Williams, Mary. *Anglo-American Isthmian Diplomacy 1815–1915*, New York, 1965.

Woodward, E. L. *Great Britain and the German Navy*, London, 1964.

Zumeta, Cesar. *Tiempo de America y de Europa 1889–1916*, Caracas, 1962.

Zumeta, Cesar. *El continente enfermo*, Caracas, 1961.

Speech of
DR JOSE ALBERTO
ZAMBRANO VELASCO
Minister of Foreign Relations
to the National Congress, 17 June, 1982

~~~

Venezuela's position over the Essequibo region is based on solid foundations and in its presentation abroad, the fullest national backing, removed from any underlying debate which might reflect random discrepancies.

This situation was accepted by England when, in 1824, upon recognising the Independence of Great Colombia, it identified the new State with the following expression: '. . . this beautiful and rich country which extends through the northern sea from the Essequibo river to the province of Guiana'.

When Schomburgh was commissioned by the English government in 1840 to perform a topographical study of Essequibian Guiana, he published a new map, reflecting Britain's maximum aspiration of the time. Landmarks were even placed along this supposed border line, produced by his imagination. Later, in 1887, another map was published in an even more expansionist mode, penetrating deeply into our country's territory.

On 17 December, 1895, the President of the United States of America stated that his country was investigating unilaterally, through an *ad hoc* commission, the status of the true divisory line which, once established, he would be obliged to defend against British claims.

During the development of these negotiations, US Secretary of State Olney hid from his own officers, from Venezuela's lawyers and from the Venezuelan government the sense and scope of the commitments which he had acquired with Great Britain. At the same time that he presented Venezuela with explanations on the meaning of certain clauses, he made commitments accepting other meanings with the Foreign Office. Thus, for example, he indicated to Venezuela one interpretation of the way in which prescription lapses would be computed, by which the *de facto* occupation could not become legitimate, while at the same time he secretly agreed with England to an entirely different method, gravely detrimental to our country.

The Russian super-arbitrator was a well-known Anglophile, supporter of the Russo-British alliance. Years before the judgment he had written that 'the future of Asia and the future fate of its possessions oblige Russia and England not to lose sight of the sublime Role which Divine Providence has imparted to them, for the good of the savage and barbarous nations of this part of the world'. Furthermore, he understood that international law 'is not applicable to relations between a civilized power and a semi-savage nation'.

The decision was ridden with flaws. It obeyed no legal principle. The decision was a political pact, which failed even to commit all the interested States, as it was performed behind Venezuela's back. At no time did it take into account or invoke the rules which had been agreed upon in the already flawed arbitral treaty.

Furthermore, the decision pronounced judgment on a subject which the arbitral court had no faculty to take up by the terms of the previous treaty, and which neither of the parties had requested. It declared, in effect, that the Amacuro and Barima Rivers were open to free navigation. This is a flaw known as *extra-petita,* which affects the entire decision.

Thus this judicial farce attempted to legitimize the despoliation undertaken by force, and to seize part of Venezuela's territory.

The strange arbitral Treaty which left Venezuela without representation was signed in 1897. Venezuela was just emerging from the ruin of a bloody civil war.

Anguish, the war among brothers, poverty to the extreme of misery, foreign intervention, political persecution, and loans of doubtful public morality but urgent necessity, became the normality of Venezuelan life.

After the Second World War, when new facts whose entire significance was previously unknown further justified Venezuela's rejection of the decision of 1899, our claim took on new vigour. The newly revealed facts indicated the precise circumstances surrounding the work of the so-called Court of Paris and allowed a clearer perception of the scope of the abuse.

At that time, under the auspices of the United Nations, the process of decolonialization was begun, giving hope to victims of colonialism that they could re-establish their territorial integrity which had been breached by imperialist expansionism.

Thus, the fact that Venezuelan proceedings in the last twenty years have been performed under the orientation of governments arising from popular sovereignty, has morally and politically reinforced the value of our fair claim.

This is a formal treaty by which the involved parties agree to seek peaceful solutions for a controversy inherited from colonialism. Said Agreement was reached through the open channel of negotiation, at which representatives of the Government of British Guiana were always present. The government of Venezuela did not wish them to be excluded, because it did not care to fall into the same errors which affected the 1899 decision and the arbitral treaty of 1897, when power plays led to political compromises in the interest of the great powers, sacrificing those of our own country.

Neither did Venezuela oppose Guiana's independence. The Venezuelan government knew that such a position could entail difficulties, but it could not renege on its consistent struggle against colonialism. Venezuela recognized Guiana's independence, clearly reserving the nation's rights to the usurped territory.

The Geneva Agreement begins by recognizing the existing controversy and establishes procedures for encountering a peaceful solution. It expressly provides that the matter should be resolved in a manner acceptable to both parties. Article I of the Agreement calls for negotiation of a 'satisfactory solution for the practical settlement of the controversy'. These elements require contemplation not only of the legal points implied in the matter, but also of all historical, moral, political, geographical, and other considerations which could lead to a balanced, practical, acceptable, and definitively fair result.

During the four years of operation of the Mixed Commission, between 1966 and 1970, Venezuela made every effort to meet with the obligation to negotiate in good faith, as defined by International Law. Our representation did everything within its reach, and took every possible initiative to see that the negotiations would be meaningful and allow some progress.

However, the representation of Guiana, rather than approaching the matter of the territorial claim in the manner in which it was legally obliged to do so, obstinately refused to consider any possibility of a practical and satisfactory solution to the matter. It limited itself to declaring that the 1899 decision was a consummate fact and that, Venezuela having not achieved its annulment, there was no further discussion.

In view of the preceeding events, it should be no surprise that the Mixed Commission during its four years of work was not able to fulfil the mission entrusted to it by the Treaty of 1966. As the Venezuelan commissioners indicated in their report of 18 June, 1970, 'the failure to meet with the Geneva Agreement is not due to failure to find a satisfactory solution for a practical settlement of the controversy, but to the fact that, in spite of Venezuela's efforts, such a solution was not even attempted'. A true standstill had been reached at that moment.

Under these difficult circumstances the Protocol of Port of Spain was signed, which temporarily suspended the application of the procedures foreseen in Article IV of the Geneva Agreement, with the intention of retaining its force and the possibility of its future constructive application under more favourable conditions.

Certainly, when analysed with full objectivity, the Protocol of Port of Spain has justified its existence. It has been made clear to the Guianese people that their permanent economic and social crisis is not due, as their government would have them believe, to supposed Venezuelan harassment. The perpetuation of the existing personalist regime in Guiana, in the midst of accusations of electoral manipulation, has erroded the initial image carefully cultivated before the international community, of a newly independent patriotic leadership dedicated to the country's defence against an envious neighbour. Venezuela's patient and serene efforts have counteracted attempts to cast it as the aggressor, and its sustained diplomatic action has revealed to the nations of the world the elemental justice of Venezuela's claim and its permanent willingness to achieve reasonable solutions through peaceful means.

The degree of relaxation achieved permitted a reopening of the dialogue during the last constitutional period. New negotiation initiatives were undertaken, reflecting the continuity of our claim. Although these negotiations were undertaken at the highest level the attitude of the government of Guiana did not aid in the conclusion of a design for a draft solution. Today Venezuela, strengthened in every aspect and with a solid and respected international record, may undertake the new process of negotiation under more favourable conditions.

On 18 June, 1982, the application of the procedure established by Article IV of the Geneva Agreement goes into effect from that date, means of solution to controversies reflected in Article 33 of the United Nations Charter are to be employed.

What are these means?

Negotiation
Investigation
Mediation
Conciliation
Arbitrage
Judicial settlement
Resource to regional organisms or agreements
Other peaceful means chosen by the parties involved

Thus talks will be opened between Guiana and Venezuela, to determine the applicable means to solution of the territorial controversy. Should three months elapse without reaching an agreement, the indication of an applicable measure will be assigned to a third party. That third party will be the international body chosen by both governments by common agreement, or should they fail so to chose, the Secretary General of the United Nations.

We approach this new phase in our territorial claim with the fullest and most constructive purpose. In that spirit, we have defined the general criteria which, as of this moment, will orient Venezuelan actions, in full keeping with the Geneva Agreement.

The means of solution chosen should adapt to the nature of the controversy and respect the details which the parties have defined to solve it, since in this phase the fundamental idea which dominates the Geneva Agreement also prevails.

To satisfy this requirement it is first necessary to fulfil faithfully the stage of direct negotiation which has not yet been carried out. The duty of negotiating in good faith is not only implanted in the Agreement itself, but is also referred to directly by Article 33 of the United Nations Charter.

It is clear that the possibilities of negotiation, which were never truly undertaken, are far from exhausted as sources of a satisfactory result to our territorial controversy.

In this sense, to initiate this new stage, we shall invite the government of Guiana to comply sincerely with the provision of Article IV of the Geneva Agreement, choosing negotiation among the means of solution mentioned in the United Nations Charter.

The national government is fully aware of the difficulties which this process will present, in view of the historical background. In spite of this circumstance, it has considered it advisable to insist on negotiation. As mentioned above, this is the method most in keeping with the purposes of the Geneva Agreement, to which we shall strictly adhere.

During these years we have witnessed tragic episodes in international relations. Some of these have arisen from a subtle exercise in violence, which Venezuela has denounced and consisting of disregard for the requirements of peaceful solutions.

The lack of a real will for the solution to problems, translated into exasperating silence, or into the mere appearance of negotiation, where verbalism, matters of style and so-called prior questions occupy space and time which should be devoted to matters of depth, leads to aggravation of the problems.

Venezuela desires a participating Guiana in the continental march towards integration. Venezuela desires a positive relationship with its neighbour. We are sure that the people of Guiana share this purpose.

We desire a Guiana whose inhabitants of every race enjoy the fullest human rights and participate in the construction of their own destiny and development.

We greet all Guianese with the conviction that a timely solution to the differences inherited from colonialism will impel our convergence towards progress and development.

Venezuela wishes above all else to win the battle of Guianese peace and brotherhood, because we are inevitably neighbours and because to a large part we are children of the same American history.

We hope that Guiana will share in the continent's causes, as we also hope the English-speaking Caribbean countries who have recently become independent will. Venezuela carries out a policy of cooperation throughout the area, inspired by the wish to strengthen continental unity.

It is necessary that the Caribbean countries make an effort to identify as part of a single continent: that effort will bear as its fruit the creation of a framework of solidarity wherein we may resolve our differences peacefully.

We are a country which has earned the respect of the international community: through our unwaivable attachment to the cause of justice and right as the axis for international relations, through our exemplary democratic regime, whose government truly represents its citizens, respects public freedoms and guarantees the enforcement of human rights; through our invariable opposition to colonialism in all its manifestations and the support we have offered those struggling to free themselves from it; through our contribution to the search for a new international economic order among Third World countries; through our repudiation of war, conquest and economic predomination as an instrument of international policy.

Venezuela's position in its fair claim to the Essequibo territory is not only the government's position: it is the position of the entire nation.

This matter and the present circumstances of Latin America call us to unity. The government hopes, Senators and Deputies, to have the solid backing of the entire Nation at every moment of the important stage now under way.

This ample presentation, before Congress, of the approaching problems, concludes with a call for national unity. The government demands it. Venezuela needs it. May God enlighten us and help us wisely and opportunely to make the decisions which our Country requires of us.

CARACAS, 17 June, 1982

Index